TEXAS
CONSTABLES

TEXAS CONSTABLES

A FRONTIER HERITAGE

ALLEN G. HATLEY

TEXAS TECH UNIVERSITY PRESS

This book is typeset in Galliard and Copperplate Gothic. The paper used in this book meets the minimum requirements of ANSI/NISO Z39.48–1992 (R1997). ∞

Designed by Tamara Kruciak

Library of Congress Cataloging-in-Publication Data
    Hatley, Allen G.
    Texas constables : a frontier heritage / Allen G. Hately.
        p. cm.
    Includes bibliographical references and index.
    ISBN 0-89672-424-7 (cloth : alk. paper)
    ISBN 0-89672-581-2 (pbk : alk paper)
    1. Constables–Texas–History. 2. Law enforcement–Texas–History. I. Title.
HV8145. T4H37 1999
363.2'09764—dc21

                                                        99-041280
                                                        CIP

ISBN-13 978-0-89672-424-2 (cloth)
ISBN-13 978-0-89672-581-2 (paperback)

Printed in the United States of America

06 07 08 09 10 11 12 13 14 / 9 8 7 6 5 4 3 2 1
SB

Texas Tech University Press
Box 41037
Lubbock, Texas 79409–1037 USA
800.832.4042
ttup@ttu.edu
www.ttup.ttu.edu

This book is dedicated to two mentors: Dr. Julia Kathryn Garrett, my high-school history teacher and author who made Texas history "the love of my life," and E. Bruce Curry, long-time district attorney of the 216th Judicial District in Texas, who gave me my initial chance in law enforcement when those in my own county would not. It is also dedicated to those Texas constables, past and present, who have often had to contend with indifferent if not hostile county governments, but have still managed to provide their constituents with a real measure of safety and justice.

The West is dead my Friend.
But writers hold the seed.
And what they sow
Will live and grow
Again to those who read.
—*C. M. Russell, 1917*

CONTENTS

CONTENTS

PREFACE

On March 5, 1823, John Tumlinson Sr., alcalde, or justice of the peace, of the newly established Colorado District in Stephen F. Austin's first colony in Texas, wrote to Baron de Bastrop in San Antonio that he had "appointed but one officer who acts in the capacity of constable to summon witnesses and bring offenders to justice." Tumlinson was referring to Thomas V. Alley, whom he had appointed as the first constable in Texas soon after Governor Trespalacios divided the colony into two districts in December 1822, for better civil administration and justice. A year later, Alley was required by newly approved civil codes to obtain a bond, which he did on January 26, 1824. That same day Constable John Austin made bond in the San Felipe de Austin District.

It should be noted that the appointment in the first month of 1823 of a constable in Stephen F. Austin's colony is no "faint beginning." It is the confirmation in what was later to become the republic and then the state of Texas that the first peace officers appointed were constables. This should surprise no one, for those were the most familiar and most active law enforcement officers known to those Anglo-Texan colonists, who mainly arrived from the southern United States.

My efforts to find out more about the history of Texas constables were touched off by a strong interest in Western history and my own involvement in law enforcement over the last decade, culminating in my election as a constable in Bandera County in 1992 and again in 1996. When I campaigned for the office, I spoke to a number of individuals and groups about the position. With few exceptions, I noted that most of those I spoke with lacked a clear understanding of the duties and the long history of Texas constables as peace officers, even though they voted for one every four years.

Much has been written about individual peace officers, and about the many federal law-enforcement agencies, various state highway patrols, the Texas Rangers, and many of the town marshals or county sheriffs from years past, but initially I found very few references to constables, except for those in Canada and England. So when I decided to write first some articles, and later a book, I gave my subject the working title, "The Constable: An Unheralded Peace Officer," then began filling the void in the history of this group of lawmen.

As I worked to document the adventures and accomplishments of Texas constables, based upon my own experience and research, it became very obvious that two powerful factors influence the way a constable performs his or her duties. First, Texas constables were and are still very much the product of their own individuality. Legendary Texas lawman, T. W. "Buckshot" Lane, who served eight years as constable in Precinct No. 1 and twelve years as sheriff, both in Wharton County, may have said it best when interviewed by Thad Sitton as part of an oral history project in 1986: "The constable had as much authority as a sheriff, only he had a small precinct. They had the same authority as the sheriff, but mainly they served papers. . . . Some constables took it on themselves to enforce the law. I enforced the law in my precinct." It is no different today. Some constables just serve papers, some are involved in providing their constituents with a good measure of safety and protection and enforce the law, while some just "smoke and joke" or drive down the highway in a fine-looking vehicle and serve little or no real law enforcement purpose.

The second factor in a constable's career is how county government operates. The attitudes and procedures employed by different Texas county governments affect a constable's job more than any constitutional provision. District and county attorneys who vigorously prosecute offenders and are not afraid to go to trial are vital to effectively enforcing the law. And although the voters may elect the constables, the commissioner's court can withhold any part of or all their salary and operating funds, sometimes making it impossible for a constable to fulfill the oath of office. Therefore, county-level political alliances, friendly ties, personality conflicts, and power struggles have a great impact on every constable's performance.

While researching this book, I realized that infusing the text with large doses of folklore would not be appropriate, so I have tried to stick to the facts by identifying and documenting the real adventures and accomplishments of many constables. I also thought it was important to describe the environments in which constables have worked and the evolution of local government from Austin's Colony through the organization of various counties. Finally, of course, the exploits and events of Texas constables needed to be placed against the backdrop of Texas, and American, history.

Many a constable has left only his name and an isolated event—often his death—to mark his place in history. Constable Bill Garsee who was murdered in Polk County in 1984, is such an individual. But there are many more. The first recorded death of a constable in the line of duty in the United States, was in Venango County, Pennsylvania, on April 14, 1825. Since then, at least 130 other constables or their deputies in twenty-nine states have died in the line of duty. In the twentieth century, Texas has lost the most, with twenty-five identified. Missouri and California follow.

Two Texas constables killed during this century died almost eight years and several hundred miles apart, but their deaths were tied to racial troubles. One of these men, James W. Mitchell, of Bell County, was killed from ambush by a black man. The other, Constable Bragg Dunbar, of Freestone County, was killed because he came to the aid of a black man. I believe that their actions and their deaths prove better than any statistic how most Texas constables have attempted through the years to dispense justice equally among their constituents.

Constable Gus Krempkau, who was killed in 1881 on the streets of El Paso, was another example of a strong proponent of justice for all. Krempkau was shot because he was outspoken in attempting to convince the court to indict the murderers of two Mexican cowboys as they searched for their stolen cattle on the north side of the Rio Grande.

This work is not a catalog of Texas constables past and present. In general, I include only those whose recognition for service I can verify. Where I was only able to find a name, I may or may not have recorded it here. The vast majority of constables in this book are included because of events or careers that single them out from their peers.

I am convinced that my background and experience as a professional law enforcement officer helped in my search for stories and in my analysis of what might have gone "right" or "wrong" on the roads traveled by the people in this book. For one thing, I knew the right questions, and in many cases the right people to ask for assistance, especially in relation to the actions of constables in the twentieth century.

Although my law enforcement experience was helpful, I found that researching historical documents could be frustrating. For example, it quickly became obvious that constables of old were elected in some jurisdictions and appointed in others, and in many cases it was impractical or impossible to distinguish between the two categories. Determining details of jurisdiction and the manner of taking office became even more problematic in other states. After a while, however, I came to realize that regardless of how these constables came to office, they all served, and they contributed to the history recorded on these pages.

It also became apparent that some constables served concurrent or overlapping terms as town marshals or deputy sheriffs, or worked in private security, during their time in office. Sometimes this caused resentment or jealousy. In addition to how a constable came to serve and in how many positions, jurisdiction itself can be a point of confusion. Even today, it is not unusual for a constable to be referred to in newspaper articles and other references simply as, "the constable in Port Aransas," or perhaps "a constable in Mansfield." In each case, the men were actually constables in county precincts—Nueces County in the case of Port Aransas and Tarrant County in the case of Mansfield.

The inherent limitation of only serving usually a rural county precinct or a small town rather than a larger jurisdiction such as an entire county, state, or nation, has contributed in many, many instances to the incompleteness of the historic record. Yet staggering exceptions loom large, as in the case of Constable Darrell Lunsford, whose murder was recorded on his patrol car video camera in 1991 during a traffic stop on Highway 59 in Nacogdoches County. His murder has been seen by millions on television.

A Texas constable comes closest to epitomizing what some law enforcement theoreticians had in mind when they began to talk about "community policing." Unfortunately, few of those providing leadership to the criminal justice system have taken the time, or made the effort to take optimum advantage of this already existing asset to the community, probably because of bias or a poor grasp of a constable's qualifications.

It is in the county precinct or local community where constables could and should make their greatest contributions today. But because of the ever-increasing effort of some politicians, bureaucrats, and law enforcement agencies to centralize the power of government, local law enforcement at the precinct level in Texas and elsewhere in the United States has suffered and is in jeopardy. Mostly these are the same legislators and politicians who have been silent for years on law-and-order issues such as aggressive prosecution, but now talk about "putting more police on the streets," a political slogan that many law-enforcement groups laugh openly about.

But when it comes to constables, who are potentially the most cost effective peace officers in a community, some politicians are too often ignorant of the office and seek to abolish it. This proves that their real interest is not in "putting more police on the street," because the average constable is as well trained and experienced as any other peace officer.

Frank Prassel's excellent review of law enforcement, entitled *The Western Peace Officer, A Legacy of Law and Order,* published in 1972 by the University of Oklahoma Press, is in my opinion a "must read" on this subject. But as good as it is, much has happened to professional law enforcement since its publication. As a result, this great book is outdated in its analysis in general of Western peace officers in small departments that at the time of publication upheld less than high standards for law enforcement. Today, however, it is more often the large law-enforcement department, usually federal, but sometimes state or county, that has lost the confidence of many of those they are sworn to serve and protect.

High standards of law enforcement in the 1990s have less to do with the size of the department than with an insistence by the voters for competence in those elected or appointed to head law-enforcement agencies in each community. This is true whether we are talking about the office of constable (each of which, in the eyes of the state, is a separate and autonomous law-enforcement agency), the police, or a sheriff's department.

In Texas over the last two decades, more demand for higher education and advanced training in law enforcement (including mandatory academy attendance, the passing of a state test no matter the law-enforcement position, and mandatory in-service training for every officer) have significantly raised professionalism and standards typical of many law enforcement agencies. This does not mean that there are no problems among law enforcement personnel today. Incompetent constables, sheriffs, and other law enforcement officers still exist. It is only necessary to review the monthly disciplinary actions taken by the Texas Commission on Law Enforcement Officer Standards and Education (TCLEOSE), which in Texas is the partial equivalent of an internal affairs department for county, precinct, and some municipal police organizations, to realize that policemen of all types still have their problems.

For those in law enforcement who wish to avoid policing a populous metropolitan area, I suggest that being a rural constable is one of the most satisfying law-enforcement jobs in Texas, assuming a competent justice of the peace and a working relationship with the sheriff and the county commissioners court. Working on a local level, a constable can often truly seek justice, while providing a real measure of safety and tranquility to his constituents. Unrealistically small budgets, a hostile courthouse, unnecessary competition among law enforcement agencies can destroy the usefulness of the position of constable just as surely as the election or appointment of an unqualified individual, but most of these problems can be solved if ego and power-seeking are minimized and a common goal is understood. The abolition of the office of constable in Texas, which some have proposed, would not significantly reduce the overall cost of government. Yet it might well increase the costs of other law enforcement agencies, concentrate police power in a small elite group, slow the court process, and take some very qualified peace officers off the street.

The ability of law enforcement agencies in the late twentieth and early twenty-first centuries to serve their constituents effectively is becoming less and less possible in many Texas communities. This is especially true where some county sheriffs have unfortunately become, owing to larger and larger county jails, little more than hotel keepers with barred windows for the drunk, the disturbed, and the criminal element within their communities.

Better utilization of and communication between the office of constable and other law enforcement agencies and county officials in any community could go a long way toward keeping the Texas constable on the street.

Lack of understanding what a constable is has led to a remarkable dearth of reference to this position, even among some writers of Western history, lore, and adventure whom we enjoy and respect. Few except those in law enforcement are actually aware of constables' role in local government, much less their role in history, even though constables are still elected by many voters across the United

States. Because these constables who are elected, work, and die outside the state of Texas are so integral to the complete picture, I include notable stories of a number of famous and not so famous constables from other regions of the country.

As the book neared completion, I discussed the title with a friend, and fellow author, who suggested *Texas Constables: A Frontier Heritage*. It seemed a perfect fit, for the Texas constable is the product of our heritage. He is also, I believe, a benefit worthy of preservation. I hope this book will inspire others to dig deeper into the history of constables in their own state or region, for there is plenty of room for more research.

I hope, too, that the stories, information, and suggestions in this book will help the reader understand what it is to be a constable, what those now holding the office are trained for, and what they are capable of doing. I also hope that other writers will begin to include constables in their stories about law enforcement.

Acknowledgments

Many people assisted the author during the research and writing of this book. It is very difficult to name everyone who helped, so forgive me if I've forgotten anyone. The book could not have been written without assistance from many people and organizations.

Over the many months this book was in preparation, I wrote, called, and visited hundreds of constables, and deputy constables in Texas and elsewhere, along with their families, and friends, and other lawmen seeking information, names, and events to help identify those who should be included in this book. Most of those in law enforcement who were called upon to assist went out of their way to help me write about some constable or deputy constable, so that person could be recognized and his life and efforts remembered. I wish especially to thank Constables David S. Crawford, Buck Bonner, Mike Honeycutt, and Jim Masur, along with Deputy Constables Gary Edwards, and T. M. Peterson, all from Texas, who went out of their way to encourage me or to assist in the research for this book. Thanks also to Constable John L. Graham, whose father Constable Allen Graham was killed in the line of duty in Pecos County in 1972, and to Constable John A. Ford, whose brother Constable Lewis O. Ford was also killed in the line of duty in Orange County in 1971, for their cooperation and assistance in completing this book, and for carrying on the tradition of Texas constables.

A special thanks to all those others who provided information, helped me compile information, or provided ideas for this book, including Shirley Lunsford, D. L. Lunsford, David Fuller, Tim James, C. R. "Chuck" Staton, Tom Walker, Teenie Garsee, Mike Nicholson, Jerry Farmer, Judge Hector Lopez, L. Anthony Page, John D. Clifton, A. J. Garsee, Borta Andrews, and Tommie Hindes. Thanks also to everyone in the Crime Records Service at the Texas Department of Public Safety, especially Pam Nickel, who went out of her way many times to help me keep this book accurate. A special thanks to Robert G. McCubbin, who so generously provided photographs of John Selman and his son John Jr., and to Dr. William Wilbanks,

Leon Metz, Rick Miller, Carbo's Police Museum in Pigeon Forge, Tennessee, and to the many others who assisted and sometimes did not even know it.

I also want to thank those who helped me locate, discover, and copy various documents, and those who offered advice in the many libraries, museums, newspapers, law-enforcement agencies, the Texas State Archives, and the Barker American History Library in Austin, Texas. I thank the National Law Enforcement Officers Memorial, who generously provided me with the names of fallen officers across the United States.

A special mention to those who always help make a book more attractive, and valuable—the photo archivists with the western history collections at the University of Oklahoma Library, the Kansas State Historical Society, Texas State Library and Archives Commission, the Panhandle-Plains Historical Museum, the Border Heritage Center at the El Paso Public Library, and the Western History Department at the Denver Public Library. They opened their files and assisted me in finding and obtaining copies of photographs at a fair price. It is unfortunate that we are often denied the same consideration from many large libraries and universities in the state of Texas.

Last but not least I wish to thank Janet Cave, who many times during the writing of this book provided advice, assistance, and occasional inspiration.

CHAPTER I
THE SPIT-DOG OF THE TREADMILL
OF GOVERNMENT

MEDIEVAL ORIGINS TO THE MAGNA CHARTA

According to scholars, the word *constable* derives apparently from the Latin *comes stabuli,* which means master of the horse, master of the stables, or count of the stables. This is because early constables in France were, in fact, military officers; their duties consisted of raising armies and local militia for the king. Other possible derivations of the title *constable* have been suggested, but that given here is by far the most accepted.[1]

Some writers claim that in medieval England, constables were members of King Alfred's household by 871 A.D., but the record shows that only a few years after William of Normandy defeated the English King Harold II on October 14, 1066, at the Battle of Hastings, constables were a major part of William the Conqueror's kingdom. By 1070, Robert d'Oilly, who was a favorite of King William I, was given his first great household office at court. D'Oilly was appointed constable of his shrievalty by William I and again by William II. In 1086, he was made sheriff of Warwickshire.[2]

To assure himself a continued reign, William the Conqueror divided England into fifty-five military districts, each called a *shire.* He placed a trusted former army officer, a *reeve,* in charge of each, and soon the head of each district was referred to as a *shire reeve*—the origin of the term *sheriff.* Constables were appointed by the crown to supervise boroughs, or individual communities within the shires. These were referred to commonly as *a hundred,* for the number of people making up the medieval English community, hence the term *precinct.*

Over the next two hundred years, many sheriffs in England were given more and more administrative duties (including the responsibility for the king's prisoners) and were decreasingly able to give

1

much attention to law enforcement and peace and order. As a result, constables assumed more and more responsibility for law enforcement in the realm. Nonetheless, lawlessness grew rampant until 1215, when the Magna Charta was forced upon King John at Runnymede on June 15. In effect, the Magna Charta made all in the realm, including the King, subject to the law. The excesses of certain court officials, particularly sheriffs, were addressed in that document: Article 45 states in part, "we will only appoint as justiciars, constables, sheriffs, or bailiffs, such as know the law of the land, and intend to observe it properly."[3]

Although the Magna Charta provided for law and order, keeping the peace became increasingly difficult in England in the latter half of the thirteenth century. Again and again sheriffs were enjoined to establish watches, to post men on guard at night, and to arrest all strangers passing through their territory at night. Constables, too, came under pressure to protect the realm, but there were sometimes problems of jurisdiction. In 1242, one well-known chief constable, who was thought to be an enemy of the king, was not allowed to act independently, and was placed under the direction of a sheriff. And in 1276, the constable in charge of Dover castle ordered the sheriff of Kent to return to his county when it was discovered he was on his way to assist in the siege of Rochester castle.[4]

After 1285, the Statute of Winchester was enacted to provide for the appointment of constables to replace bailiffs. Constables in England were not recognized as employees of boroughs, counties, or the crown. Instead, they were considered professional citizens: responsible only to their communities or constituents, they were charged with dispensing justice and maintaining law and order,[5] and were paid a portion of the fees they collected.

By the seventeenth century, local government was well established in England, and sheriffs and constables were the tax collectors of the king. By this time, high constables, assisted by petty constables, were established throughout the country, and were the primary law-enforcement officers and tax collectors within a precinct.[6]

CONSTABLES COME TO AMERICA

Although the first permanent colony established by the English in North America was at Jamestown in 1607, it was not until the 1620s that the Chesapeake Colonies, as Virginia and later Maryland were first called, began to think about local government. In Virginia, *the hundreds,* groups of plantations with sometimes ill-defined boundaries, formed the first local units of government, before the establishment of counties in 1634. In Maryland, even after the first counties were formed in 1651, the hundred continued to serve, within the county, as a fiscal, military, and, for a time, representational unit.[7]

Constables in the Virginia Colony were well established by the 1640s, serving much the same duties as constables elected today in the state of Texas. This is evident from the actual oath of office for constables, contained in the records of Accomac[k] County, Virginia, for the years 1640 to 1645:

> You shall swear that you shall well and truly serve Our Sovereign Lord the King in the Office of a Constable. You shall see and cause his Majesties peace to be well and duly kept and performed according to your power within your limit. You shall arrest all such persons as in your sight and presence shall commit or make any affray, riot, or other breach of his Majesties peace.
>
> You shall do your best endeavor upon complaint to you made to apprehend all felons, malicious persons, revolutionists or persons riotously assembled, and if any such offender shall make resistance with force, you shall summon assistance (hue and cry) from the citizens of the community, and shall pursue them to the utmost of your limit and give warning to the next Constable for his or their pursuing.
>
> You shall have a watchful eye on such persons as shall keep any food or provisions, and drinking houses, and to all such as shall unlawfully frequent such places. You shall well and duly execute all Acts of Assembly to which the said Acts command you, as also all Writs and Warrants to you directed from the Governor or any of the Council, or any of the Commissioners for the Monthly Courts, within your jurisdiction. And you shall well and duly, according to your knowledge, power, and ability do and execute all other things belonging to the office of a Constable, so long as you shall continue in this office, so help you God.[8]

By the 1650s, the colonies of Virginia and Maryland differed very little structurally in their local government. A commissioner (essentially a justice of the peace), a coroner, a county clerk, and the sheriff were the important county officials. The chief qualifications for the office of sheriff were the same in Maryland and Virginia, as they were in England, "that he be of sufficient estate." As a result, the choice was restricted to the group of planters in each county. These large landowners monopolized all of the major county offices in most American colonies, and at times even served as high constables and deputy surveyors. Because most of the county offices held were tied to money and not duty, constables in most precincts of the Chesapeake colonies were usually the most active law-enforcement officers.[9]

The primary duties of both sheriffs and constables in this period were to supervise elections, collect taxes and fees for service, maintain lists, and provide notice of government acts and directives, and then to keep the peace, and arrest lawbreakers. In Virginia, the Act of 1661–62 provided for a systematic census taking, primarily for the purpose of collecting taxes and for elections. It was at this time that Virginia counties were first divided into precincts. The constables and justices of the peace contacted people and made up the lists.[10]

Constables also served in the other British colonies. They were part of the law-enforcement community in Massachusetts by 1660 and by 1676 were in service in colonial New York. There, in 1692, constables were ordered to maintain a "good pair of stocks . . . in every town within Kings County, and to [keep them] . . . in sufficient repair." The relationships between justices of the peace and constables were very close at the time, and formalized in the pursuit of law and order.[11]

Constables in colonial America sometimes failed to perform their duties, and they suffered the consequences. For example, in 1706 in Brooklyn, New York, Constable Jacob Fardon "failed to summon all the inhabitants of Brooklyn to a town meeting." We know this because when "two freeholders swore they were not summoned to the meeting," Fardon was fined five pounds and another person was appointed in his place.[12]

No better final comment regarding constables' duties and their importance in the original thirteen colonies can be made than that by Julius Goebel and T. Raymond Naughton, in *Law Enforcement in Colonial New York: A Study of Criminal Procedure (1664-1776)*:

the Constable is, of course, the spit-dog of the treadmill of government. His is the arduous task of serving precepts which may issue from any part of the province; he must attend not only the annual Assizes [County Court], but his presence is required at his town court

4

and he must not fail to be present with his staff [badge of office] at the Sessions. The business of collecting rates is upon him, and he does the distraining of the recalcitrant. He must pursue the fleeing malfactor, and he must present him. In company with the overseers he may have to examine persons for the Sessions or for the Council. Whatever a justice of the peace may wish to pass on to him the Constable cannot avoid. Even his house is no sacred castle, for the law provides that he must give sanctuary to the distracted wives of his bailiwick. Small wonder that scruples against taking the oath were often discovered.[13]

What better description of a constable's work and problems, even in the twentieth century?

CHAPTER II
TEXAS BEFORE INDEPENDENCE, 1820 TO 1836

MOSES AUSTIN'S DREAM

The death of Moses Austin was a shock to all concerned. In late 1820, only a few months before his death, he had ridden with his servant and several prospective colonists for almost eight hundred miles, from the family home in Missouri to the town of San Antonio de Bexar in Spanish Texas. Even though Austin had only fifty dollars in his pocket, he went to Texas to convince the Spanish governor that he was capable of colonizing a large grant of land with Anglo-American settlers. Moses Austin was lucky to run across an old friend while in San Antonio, the influential Baron de Bastrop, who introduced him to various government officials and helped him prepare his applications. In January 1821, Spain granted Moses Austin his colony, and he returned home in March. But within two months of Austin's return to Missouri, he died as a result of the hardships of the trip.[1]

Although initially he lacked his father's passion for colonization in Texas, Stephen F. Austin traveled to Texas after his father's death, and in August 1821, Governor Martinez recognized him as Moses Austin's heir and successor. Stephen Austin then proceeded to explore the land between the Brazos and the Colorado Rivers, selected the areas he wished to colonize, and proceeded with plans to bring the first Anglo-American colonists to Texas.[2]

At this time, there were only three important settlements in Texas. One was San Antonio de Bexar, where the army's payroll was almost the only significant source of pesos. The second was Presidio de la Bahia, or Goliad, a community that Austin describes in his diary as where the people "live poorly, have but little furniture," and "eat with forks and spoons and their fingers." The combined

Photo of a painting in Potosi, Missouri, Courthouse identified as Moses Austin. There is some doubt about the identity (courtesy Texas State Library and Archives Commission).

Stephen F. Austin. Copied from an original painting by William Howard made in 1833 while Austin was in Mexico City (courtesy Texas State Library and Archives Commission).

population of San Antonio and Goliad was less than three thousand. The third settlement was the town of Nacogdoches in East Texas, which once was fairly prosperous, but by 1821 had been nearly deserted, except for a few squatters, some Indians, and a small army garrison.[3]

In October 1821, Austin appointed Josiah H. Bell as a provisional alcalde, or justice of the peace, for his first settlers, who arrived on the Brazos in November of that year. But in late 1821, as Austin proceeded with his colonization plans, the popular revolution in Mexico that had sputtered on for more than ten years finally succeeded in gaining independence of the Spanish crown, which for almost a century had tried unsuccessfully to colonize the area north of the Rio Grande. At first, the revolution in Mexico did not greatly concern Stephen F. Austin, for he reasoned that conditions under a Mexican government would favor colonization in Texas as much as they had under a Spanish one.[4]

Nevertheless, the revolution did manage to delay further colonization of Austin's colony. Consequently in 1822 he made the long trip to Mexico City and obtained a decree in February 1823 confirming his grant. As Austin had anticipated, the new Mexican government eventually favored his ideas because not enough colonists were entering Texas from Mexico to develop an economy that would eventually pay taxes. But there were two additional factors in Texas that strongly favored further colonization by any nationality.

One of these was the desire to eliminate the Indians who had raided throughout Texas for centuries, and still rode fully armed even into San Antonio de Bexar whenever they chose. The other concern was the belief by many in the Mexican government that a land colonized by Anglo-Americans who had sworn allegiance to Mexico and were of good character, mostly married, and living peacefully in their own homes would buffer any invasion by filibusters who would someday try to take that land away from Mexico.

LAW ENFORCEMENT IN THE COLONY

The Austin Colony was subject to most of the laws and regulations of Mexico, and its governance was largely ignored by the Mexican government for several years. In December 1822, while Austin was in Mexico City, Governor José Felix Trespalacios had divided Austin's colony into two districts; one on the Colorado River, the other on the Brazos. That same month, elections were held in each district for an alcalde, who would provide better administration, justice, and military control. John Tumlinson Sr. was elected to the position in the Colorado District, and Josiah Bell was elected alcalde in the Brazos District. Before March 1823, John Tumlinson Sr. then appointed the first law enforcement officer in Austin's colony—Constable Thomas V. Alley—to "summon witnesses" and "bring offenders to justice."[5]

While Austin was in Mexico in 1823, the Mexican government confirmed his authority to "wage war against the Indians," preserve good order, and govern the colony in all civil, judicial, and military matters, according to the best of his ability.[6] In 1823, several Indian tribes living near the growing settlements of Anglo-Americans fought among themselves and with the colonists. On July 6, 1823, John Tumlinson was on his way to San Antonio to consult with Baron de Bastrop and Governor Trespalacios on several legal and court matters as well as the escalating Indian problems when he was attacked and killed by Indians. He was replaced by James Cummins.[7]

When Austin returned to his colony from Mexico City on August 4, 1823, he found great pessimism among the first colonists who had waited for his return. Because of Indian problems, few additional colonists were entering Texas. Even two years later, the census of 1825 showed only 1,825 persons in the colony, almost twenty percent of which were slaves. By 1831, the number had increased to 5,665. On January 22, 1824, Stephen F. Austin promulgated a set of "Instructions and Regulations for the Alcaldes," a brief civil and criminal code of justice that Austin had written upon his return from Mexico City in 1823, and which had been approved by the Mexican government.

The criminal portion of the code dealt primarily with offenses by and against Indians and slaves. The civil portion of the code provided for appointment of a sheriff to execute his own process, and constables to execute those of the alcaldes. A fee structure was also laid out whereby the alcalde, sheriff, and constables were paid for performing civil and criminal duties. Soon after adopting the code, Austin appointed one sheriff for the entire colony. Apparently the sheriff took little action, probably because of the distance between settlements. In fact, it was not until June 1825 that the sheriff was called upon to subpoena several witnesses regarding the serious matter of sedition and keeping the public peace. The sheriff later arrested A. C. Buckner, the man charged with those crimes.[8] In Austin's colony, most of the real power resided with the alcaldes and constables in their districts, or with Austin himself. The major exceptions were capital criminal cases, which had to be referred to the central government for final disposition.

By the time the criminal code had been adopted, Austin's colony already had two law enforcement officers—both constables. Their names were Thomas V. Alley and John Austin (supposedly no relation to Stephen F.). They served the colony well, but both died before Texas fought its revolution with Mexico.

Thomas V. Alley was listed as a farmer, single, and twenty-five years of age in the 1823 census of the Colorado District. He had come to Texas from Missouri in 1822 as one of the "Old Three Hundred" colonists in Stephen Austin's first colony. Alley's record in Texas history is brief, however: while on a campaign against the Waco and Tonkawa Indians in the spring of 1826, he drowned crossing the flooded Colorado River when his horse fell and he was washed away.[9]

John Austin had a longer career. Not only did he serve as constable, but he became one of the colony's major business leaders. Even though John Austin and Stephen F. Austin were apparently not related, both Austins had family ties to Connecticut and became good friends and close business associates.

John Austin came to Texas in 1819, as part of Dr. James Long's three hundred armed freebooters who gathered in Louisiana "to invade Texas and establish a Republic." Long's Expedition captured Nacogdoches and Goliad. Austin became captain of a company in Long's Expedition and was captured and taken to Mexico when Long's army was defeated in Goliad two years later. Released from prison in 1821, he made his way back to the United States. Dr. Long was later captured, transported to Mexico City, and executed. After Long's death, John Austin joined the Old Three Hundred.[10]

Between 1823 and 1828, Stephen F. Austin further subdivided his first colony into a total of seven districts. In each district was an alcalde and a constable, with no other civil officers appointed. The constables in Austin's colony served civil and criminal subpoenas, criminal arrest warrants, and writs of attachment and execution, along with various citations not much different than those served today. They also brought "offenders to justice." Each was required to post bond before taking office.

Precedence for the appointment of constables in Austin's colony and the use of civil and criminal papers came from laws in the United States. For example, in 1800, the frontier state of Kentucky published a 252-page book entitled *The General Instructor: or the Office, Duties and Authority of Justices of the Peace, Sheriffs, Coroners and Constables in the State of Kentucky.* The book defined the state's penal code and listed the code of criminal procedures; it is strikingly similar to much of today's Texas Criminal Procedures.[11]

A look at one of the alcalde's court dockets for the year 1824 indicates that it was a very limited court, with both arbitration and judgments rendered in several civil small-claims proceedings but not in any criminal proceedings. The Old Three Hundred were a remarkable group of mostly law abiding citizens.[12]

In April 1825, James Strange was elected constable for the San Jacinto District. Strange, another member of the Old Three Hundred, had moved to Texas in 1822. The census of 1826 classifies Constable Strange as a farmer and stock raiser. Also an artist of some note, James Strange would sculpt busts of President Antonio López de Santa Anna and General Juan N. Almonte after their 1836 capture at San Jacinto.[13]

In 1825, Constable Strange was asked to serve a writ of execution and investigate the status of a ship called the *Schooner Mary,* which was in some danger of running aground at Red Fish Bar on the San Jacinto River. Apparently Constable Strange appointed R. M. Cartwright as his deputy constable to assist him in this matter. On May 21, Deputy Cartwright was ordered by the alcalde Humphrey Jackson to seize and sell at public sale the property of Captain Benjamin Carico on board the *Schooner Mary,* which by this time had been purposely run ashore. The seizure was ordered to satisfy the judgment against Carico. Within a short time, however, Jackson writes that in his opinion, Deputy Cartwright may have been "too premature" in his seizure, apparently because Cartwright did not give Captain Carico ten days to appeal before service of the execution. But Jackson adds that he is uncertain about the law on this point. Deputy Constable Cartwright informed Jackson that he had left the seized property aboard the *Schooner Mary,* and that he appointed "two young men to guard and take care of the schooner and cargo," but that some of the flour and whiskey were ruined. He stated that the reason for the quick sale was to avoid more expenses. A few days later, Stephen F. Austin interceded, stopped the sale, and allowed

Captain Carico to argue his case. Although the record is not clear as to Austin's decision in the matter, two days later one of the plaintiffs accused Captain Carico of illegally taking most of the seized property off the *Schooner Mary* to avoid paying the judgment. In such cases, constables sometimes see little change in their work today as compared with that 176 years ago.[14]

During 1827, the Mexican government included in its new constitution the Spanish system of ayuntamiento (often translated as a municipality but more accurately comparable to an American county because it included both urban and surrounding rural areas). Each colony in Texas was ordered to adopt this form of government by early 1828. The ayuntamiento included elected officials to administer civil and criminal affairs in each municipality, as well as other elected officials in districts or precincts with populations of at least 500 inhabitants.[15]

Between 1827 and 1834, Stephen F. Austin tried to establish a system of law that would be familiar to his colonists, yet could be included in the Mexican system. What he did in effect was establish ayuntamientos as the local councils or commissioners courts of the late 1820s and 1830s. It was not an easy fit. Trial by jury for all who wanted it, final disposition of cases within a reasonable period of time, and the ability to set bail for most offenses and get out of jail while awaiting either trial or final adjudication—common components of Anglo-American law—were unknown in Mexico at the time.[16]

With the imposition of the ayuntamiento system for governing civil law, the settlers in each of Austin's colonies now elected a new alcalde, who acted more as county judge than justice of the peace. There were also two regidors and a *sindico procurador* in each district. The duties of these last two offices are not clearly defined in Mexican law. Regidors appear to closely resemble today's city and county commissioners, and the *sindico procurador* was equivalent to a combined notary and municipal attorney. In New Mexico some twenty years later, the Mexican system had evolved to include the *soto-alguacil,* a position equivalent to constable. The sheriff's equivalent was called the *alguacil mayor.*[17]

In each new district within a colony's ayuntamiento was a *comisario,* a sort of a justice of the peace, who also took the census, kept track of those entering and leaving the precinct or district, assisted in tax collections, and executed the orders of the ayuntamiento. A district or precinct sindico seems to be closest to what

Austin's colonists thought was a constable as it was defined during the first five years of the colony or back home in Kentucky, Arkansas, or Missouri.[18] The minutes of the ayuntamiento of San Felipe de Austin, between 1828 to 1832, identify a man named Shubael Marsh, who was sworn in as constable or sindico for the new district of Victoria.[19]

THE SEEDS OF REBELLION

By 1834, there were some twenty thousand Anglo-Americans and an estimated two thousand slaves in Texas. Just two years later, on the eve of the 1836 rebellion, the number of Anglo-Americans had grown to more than thirty thousand. This boom in immigration occurred because Texas contained some of the best farm land available in the West, and even though Indians sometimes roamed the land, safety and order were relatively greater than in many other areas beyond the Mississippi. Most immigrants were from Louisiana, Kentucky, Alabama, Tennessee, Mississippi, Georgia, and the Carolinas, but some had come from Connecticut, Bavaria, Ireland, or New York. As the names and origins of those counted as the heroes of the Alamo prove, "Gone To Texas" was more than just a funny motto to thousands of adventurous, and mostly hell-raising young men with a gun, and time on their hands in the mid-1830s. To that generation, Texas was both the frontier and the future.

Stephen F. Austin was the first and most successful, but not the only, empresario with a land grant to bring mostly Anglo-American settlers to Texas. By 1828, Austin had four separate colonies in the same region of Texas. Between 1824 and 1834, a dozen others founded new colonies mostly in and around the present-day towns of Victoria, Gonzales, and Nacogdoches. The Anglo-American colonies of Austin, DeWitt, and others covering most of Texas east of San Antonio de Bexar very much resembled most any town or rural area in Louisiana, Tennessee, Alabama, or Missouri in the 1830s. It was only a matter of time before the freedoms and relative prosperity of the colonist settlements would come into conflict with the Mexican government.

On April 6, 1830, Mexico's Congress passed the Colonization Law, which alienated most Anglo settlers already in Texas. Besides halting Anglo-American immigration into Texas, it canceled all empresario contracts for colonists not already fulfilled. Further plans provided for shipping convicts to Texas from Mexican prisons. Anglo-American settlers suddenly found it impossible to have their families join them in Texas and feared that Texas might become a penal colony of Mexico.[20]

The first armed demonstrations by Anglo-American settlers took place in 1832 at Velasco, near the mouth of the Brazos River. The incident began as a reaction to the Colonization Law and the collection of new customs duties. Also stirring unrest were the imposition of martial law—with arrest and imprisonment at the whim of the Mexican Army—and the military revolt and resulting political anarchy taking place in Mexico. John Austin, the former constable in San Felipe, commanded the Texan forces in the Battle of Velasco. The fight shed blood of both Mexican troops and Anglo-American settlers, and was the first real indication that, sooner or later, Anglo-American settlers would not abide Mexican military oppression.[21]

During this time a lucky meeting took place in Matamoros, Mexico, when Stephen F. Austin, who was again returning to Texas from another visit to Mexico, met Mexican Army Colonel José Antonio Mexia. Mexia had been sent with four hundred men by the government to investigate the troubles around Velasco. It is truly a measure of the chaos in Mexico, and Mexico's poor communication with Texas, that the attack on Mexican troops by Anglo-American settlers did not immediately elicit an expedition to punish those in the Austin colonies who took part in the fighting.

Before his arrival in Texas, Colonel Mexia had come under the influence of Stephen F. Austin. Upon arrival, he sent a letter to John Austin, who then swore to remain loyal to Mexico if Mexican representatives would stop oppressing the colonists. Soon after that a group of colonists including John Austin met with Mexia at Velasco. Instead of coming ashore to do battle, Colonel Mexia entered the colony as a friend. Mexia's visit to Texas actually ended up as a recruiting trip for support of General Santa Anna, who was fighting for supremacy in Mexico, and had pledged to support the Mexican Constitution of 1824, to which most Anglo-Americans also pledged support.[22]

Soon after the Battle of Velasco, John Austin was elected brigadier general of the Texas Militia and alcalde of the San Felipe District. In August 1832, a convention of Anglo-American settlers was called, and Stephen F. Austin was elected to take a petition to Mexico to secure relief from customs duties and to request changes

Antonio López de Santa Anna (courtesy Texas State Library and Archives Commission).

in the Colonization Law of April 6th, as well as a political separation of Texas from the state of Coahuila. Before Stephen F. Austin left for Mexico, he met with John Austin, who with Robert Williams was to manage his personal business until his return.[23]

On January 19, 1833, while Stephen F. Austin was in Mexico City, General Santa Anna was installed as president of Mexico. Austin worked for almost six months, but was basically unsuccessful in obtaining any concessions from the new government, other than cancellation of the prohibition on new colonists from the United States. Austin was very disappointed, but decided that a request coming from a predominantly Mexican community might reduce the resistance to a separate state, now believed by the Mexican government to be only an Anglo-American plan. He wrote to the ayuntamiento of San Antonio de Bexar, recommending they, too, ask for a separate state for Texas. But the ayuntamiento sent a copy of the letter to Mexico City, and in May 1833, Stephen F. Austin was arrested, ostensibly for treason, and thrown into jail without ever being formally charged.[24]

Further complicating matters, in August, John Austin died of cholera, the victim of an epidemic that had begun in India in 1826 and swept through Europe and then Mexico, and into Texas. The death of John Austin concerned many, for Texas was robbed of an outstanding leading citizen.[25]

Despite his imprisonment and other disappointments, Austin's persuading the Mexican government to allow more settlers into Texas was not insignificant. It is worth noting that in 1832, Dr. John Charles Beales and James Grant obtained a new grant from Mexico for an area far to the west of any other Anglo-American settlement, between the Rio Grande and the Nueces River, in present-day Kinney County.[26]

Beales initially brought some fifty-nine Irish, German, American, Spanish American, and French colonists to his colony at Las Moras Creek. They arrived at the site of their settlement, La Villa de Dolores (which was named for Beales's Mexican wife and was near the present site of Brackettville) on March 12, 1834. They soon elected the following officials: John Beales, alcalde; W. G. Egerton, and V. Pepin, first and second regidor, respectively; and Eduard Ludecus, their sindico or constable. Ludecus wrote a series of letters to Germany during this time, describing his journey in Texas. The letters were translated into English and later published.[27]

Even though an additional group of colonists arrived later, within two years, Beales's colony was abandoned owing to a host of reasons, including the lack of rain, poor soil for crops without irrigation, Indian raids, the remoteness of the colony, and the beginning of the revolution against the Mexican government by the Anglo-American settlers. In addition, the colonists themselves appeared not to have been well suited for such harsh conditions. The last to leave the colony, in 1836, told of hiding for several days in the brush when they heard that the army led by Santa Anna was passing by on the road to San Antonio.

While Stephen F. Austin was in jail in Mexico City, two events occurred that altered Anglo-Texas colonists' attitude toward the new Mexican government. Santa Anna suddenly repudiated the Constitution of 1824, and in May 1835 he suppressed a rebellion in the Mexican state of Zacatecas. As a result, some two thousand people were killed during the fighting; and murders, rapes, and robberies were perpetrated on the citizens as punishment. This event was not easily forgotten by Austin or the Anglos and Tejanos living in Texas.[28]

Stephen F. Austin was finally released from jail in a general amnesty in 1835, two years after he went to Mexico. Upon his return to Texas in August of that year, Austin's attitude toward union with Mexico had changed completely. He had lost his confidence in Mexico's government and openly supported a revolution. The Mexican government was proceeding to increase their army garrisons in much of Texas by four thousand troops, and transferring new military leaders to Texas, including Santa Anna's brother-in-law. The "War Party" in the Anglo-American colony was also gaining more and more followers, and was agitating for revolution.

As a result, a general council was formed in Anglo-Texas, with representatives coming from most of the districts in the American colonies. The general council met in November and December 1835 and wrote a series of ordinances and decrees, some of which became the forerunner of the Texas Constitution. On January 22, 1836, James Robinson, who was called the acting governor of Texas, signed a series of these ordinances and decrees, providing for alcaldes and commissioners to appoint constables as a part of the new government of Texas. This was two months before the Texas Constitution was drafted.[29]

David Burnet, provisional governor of Texas, from an original oil painting by William Henry Huddle (courtesy Texas State Library and Archives Commission).

The office of sheriff was mentioned by the general council, but no authority to establish such an office was specified. The general council did, however, include in their ordinances and decrees authority to establish a corps of rangers, as a part of the Texas Army, to defend the northern frontier against hostile Indians. The ranger force was finally organized on March 31, 1836.[30]

The Texas revolution began in late 1835, when the Mexican Army demanded that the town of Gonzales give up the six-pound brass cannon used to defend that community against Indian attack. On October 2, 1835, Mexican dragoons coming to take the cannon were attacked by a group of Anglo-American Texans fighting under the "come and take it" flag. Many Texas settlers, both Anglo-American immigrants and Mexican-born citizens, took up arms; and the revolution was afoot. Over the next few months, revolutionary Texan forces captured Goliad, Mission Concepción south of San Antonio de Bexar, and finally San Antonio itself.

In San Antonio, Santa Anna's brother-in-law, General Martín Perfecto de Cos, surrendered to the revolutionaries on December 11, 1835. The general and his troops promised not to return to Texas, and were allowed to march south toward Mexico, with enough arms to protect themselves from hostile Indians, and to guard several hundred convicts already sent to Texas in the Mexican Army.[31]

During the first few months of 1836, civil administration in Texas was in chaos, but the Texas Constitution was signed at the site of the Constitutional Convention at Washington on the Brazos. David G. Burnet was elected interim president, and Lorenzo de Zavala vice president.

After the revolutionary Texas army was defeated at Goliad and the Alamo, most of the colonists packed up and rode or walked east toward Louisiana. The revolutionary government in Texas also fled eastward from Washington on the Brazos. The Texas Army, now led by General Sam Houston, followed in retreat.

Finally at San Jacinto on April 21, 1836, after Santa Anna foolishly divided his forces, the revolutionary army under Sam Houston attacked, slaughtered that part of the Mexican Army and captured Santa Anna, whom a month later signed two peace treaties. The war was over, and Texas had gained its freedom, but peace was decades away for most of the people of Texas.[32]

Independence Hall, site of Constitutional Convention at Washington on the Brazos in 1836; photograph taken several years later (courtesy Texas State Library and Archives Commission).

CHAPTER III

THE REPUBLIC OF TEXAS, 1836 TO 1845

Sec. 12: There shall be appointed for each county, a convenient number of justices of the peace, one sheriff, one coroner, and a sufficient number of constables, who shall hold their offices for two years, to be elected by the qualified voters of the district or county, as congress may direct. Justices of the peace and sheriffs shall be commissioned by the president.

Constitution of the Republic of Texas, March 17, 1836

NEITHER RECOGNITION NOR ANNEXATION

On March 17, 1836, just thirty-six days before independence was actually won with the defeat and capture of Santa Anna at the Battle of San Jacinto, the Constitution of the Republic of Texas was signed at Washington on the Brazos. Article IV, Section 12 of the constitution included provision for constables, justices of the peace, a coroner, and a sheriff as a part of each county government in the Republic of Texas.[1]

But in 1836, Texas had more pressing problems than what type of local or county government to install. Soon after the April 21 Battle of San Jacinto, Texas Army General Sam Houston journeyed to New Orleans to receive better medical treatment and recuperate from the leg wound he received when his second horse was shot out from under him at San Jacinto. With Houston away, the government of Texas fell into chaos. As a captive, Santa Anna signed both a peace treaty and a second treaty, wherein Mexico recognized an independent Texas, on May 14, 1836. But a large Mexican Army was still on the Rio Grande and no farther away from populated areas than a two-week march.[2]

There were no banks in Texas, no improved roads, few if any organized schools, not many doctors, and very little money in

Sam Houston, first president of the Republic of Texas (courtesy Western History Collections, University of Oklahoma Library).

circulation. In the early years of the republic, Texas operated primarily with a barter economy. The government of Texas was more than a million dollars in debt. The republic's army had actually grown with the defeat of Santa Anna, but almost all of the real veterans of the fighting had gone home to their families to plant crops that spring. As a result, by June 1836, recent arrivals from the United States and Europe made up most of the Texas Army.[3]

The biggest blow to Texans during those first months of independence was the apparent unwillingness of the government of the United States to recognize the independence of the Republic of Texas, and the hesitancy to consider annexation seriously. Representatives from Texas including Stephen F. Austin were in Washington, D.C., even before the Battle of San Jacinto, but it became increasingly clear to Texans that the U.S. government believed they would have to go to war with Mexico if Texas were annexed, and in 1836 they were just not ready for a war over Texas.

The sentiment of private U.S. citizens was different. The populace, particularly in Louisiana, Tennessee, and Mississippi, sent money, materiel, and volunteers to fight for Texas, even before the outcome of San Jacinto was known. A few banks and private individuals also loaned money to the Texas government. But Mexico still refused to recognize Texas's independence, and three months after his capture, President Santa Anna was still a prisoner in Texas.

On July 23, 1836, the provisional president of Texas, David G. Burnet, signed a proclamation calling for Texas to ratify the March 17 Constitution, elect a constitutional government, and confirm their desires for annexation. On October 3, Texas voters elected Sam Houston president of the Republic of Texas by more than seventy-five percent of the vote. Mirabeau Buonaparte Lamar, another hero of San Jacinto, was elected vice president. The Texas Constitution was ratified, and Texas voters approved annexation by the United States by a vote of 3,277 to 91. Still the United States refused to annex Texas.[4]

Stephen F. Austin, called by many the father of Texas, received less than ten percent of the vote for President. But Austin, whom President Houston immediately appointed secretary of state, was a very sick man whose health had been broken when he was jailed for almost two years in Mexico City. He would die a few months later in what would become the town of Columbia, an early capital of Texas, just two days after Christmas in 1836, barely two months past his forty-third birthday.[5]

In early 1836, there had been twenty-three ayuntamientos in Mexican Texas. Soon after Texas won its independence, the Mexican ayuntamientos system of government was abandoned throughout Texas for something more familiar to the predominantly Anglo-Texas settlers. In 1840, the Texas Congress officially adopted the English Common Law system and a county government similar in organization to those then existing in the southern United States. The capital was moved from Columbia to the new town named for General Houston that was being built on Buffalo Bayou.[6]

The Texas Constitution of March 17, 1836, created twenty-three original municipalities. These were later referred to as counties, and all were located east of San Antonio except for that town's own Bexar County. Only three of the original twenty-three counties (Harris, Sabine, and San Augustine) did not change their boundaries appreciably from those originally surveyed. Most counties were much larger than they finally were several years or a decade or more later, as new counties were carved out and organized from the land given the original Texas counties. Nacogdoches County, for example, when first organized, contained land that eventually spawned all or a large part of more than twenty-five counties along the Red River and in East Texas. The original Milam County contained all the land that would finally include the present-day towns of Mineral Wells, Abilene, Waco, Killeen, Temple, Georgetown, Giddings, and Corsicana. Bexar County contained land that would finally be divided into more than a hundred counties.[7]

The twenty-three original counties in Texas were: Austin, Bexar, Brazoria, Colorado, Goliad, Gonzales, Harrisburg, Jackson, Jasper, Jefferson, Liberty, Matagorda, Milam, Mina, Nacogdoches, Red River, Refugio, Sabine, San Augustine, San Patricio, Shelby, Victoria, and Washington. The names of two of those counties changed while Texas was still a republic. In 1837, Mina County changed its name to Bastrop, and Harrisburg was shortened to Harris in December 1839.[8]

What to do with Santa Anna was finally solved in January 1837, when the general, who had been transported to Washington D.C., was sent to Vera Cruz, Mexico. Upon his return, Santa Anna "retired" and Anastasio Bustamante became president of Mexico.

On March 3, 1837, the United States recognized the Republic of Texas in a rider on a general appropriations bill that was signed into law the next day by President Andrew Jackson, just hours before he left office. Recognition by the United States had taken almost a year, something that no Texan would have anticipated at the start of the rebellion.[9] Yet as long as Texas claimed the Rio Grande as its southwestern boundary, Mexico would not recognize its independence.

Organizing the Government

After the ratification of the Texas Constitution in late 1836, local or county government in most areas began to organize very slowly. County seats were named in most of the twenty-three original Texas counties in 1837 or 1838, and some officials were elected or appointed. But Texans were not anxious to impose a large local government on themselves, and in several of the original Texas counties (Jasper, Refugio, Shelby, and Washington) no officials are recorded as having been elected until 1839.[10]

By 1839 or 1840, however, most of the original counties had elected numerous county officials. Initially counties were run by an appointed chief justice of a county court (the governing body of a county) and elected justices of the peace. After 1841, the office of chief justice was also elective. In addition, a county clerk (who was also the treasurer), a coroner, a sheriff or tax collector, and a notary and constable for each precinct were authorized. Years later, just before Texas became a state, the composition of the county court changed; elected county commissioners replaced justices of the peace. In addition, county courts were authorized to appoint a tax assessor.

The Texas Legislature began to appoint new positions as well, including a surveyor in each county.[11] It also created the position called medical sensor, which was established by law on December 14, 1837. "Elected by joint vote of both Houses of Congress" from physicians living in a district comprising several counties, the medical sensor granted medical licenses to those desiring to practice medicine in the Republic of Texas. The position was abolished in 1848, and records of sensors' activities have not survived.[12]

As the individual counties organized, it was only natural that Nacogdoches County, a major gateway to the region and one of the areas longest occupied by Anglo-Texans, would be one of the first to hold elections for a large spectrum of offices. People in the county were often politically active. The first constables in the Republic of Texas were elected in Nacogdoches County on May 12, 1838. These men were William Chissum, E. Fitzgerald, E. E. Hamilton, and A. Waters. The precincts in which they served were not noted in election records.[13]

During the ten years of the Texas republic, there appear to have been thirty-eight constables elected in twelve Texas counties. Most were elected in 1839 or later. The greatest number of constables— thirteen—were elected in Harris County. Harris also appears to have been the most organized of the Texas counties, as all thirteen constables were assigned designated district or beat numbers. Nacogdoches County elected the second largest number, a total of nine constables; and ten other Texas counties elected the remaining sixteen.[14]

One constable whom history records in some detail was physician Elliott McNeil Millican, appointed in 1839 in Washington County, where there had apparently been no constables on the ballot. In 1843, when Brazos County was organized from part of Washington County, Millican was first appointed and then elected to the office of sheriff. Shortly thereafter, in 1844, Millican was elected representative of Brazos County to the republic's Congress. And when Texas became a state, the former constable was elected representative from Brazos County to the first, second, and third Texas Legislatures. He was then elected twice as senator, but because of a major epidemic of cholera and a lack of doctors, he returned to Brazos County to devote himself to his medical practice until he died of cholera himself October 13, 1860.[15]

In the republic, court records indicate that most of the indictments returned were for gambling. If the Old Three Hundred before the revolution were for the most part a nonviolent people, the act of murder, except by hostile Indians or Mexican bandits, was just as rare after independence. The only exceptions were when bands of horse and cattle thieves entered Texas from Arkansas or Louisiana. At one time or another during the republic, the criminal code prescribed death for theft of horses or certain other property and for robbery. Whipping and branding were sometimes authorized for extreme cases of larceny.[16]

The first Congress passed laws making fourteen offenses punishable by death. Public lashings were also popular, but jail time of more than a year was rare. In East Texas, there were also several violent, ongoing feuds between families of fugitives and lawbreakers from the United States that had long inhabited this part of Texas. One group of thugs gained control of the Shelby County government in the early days of the republic and gave themselves and friends immunity from prosecution. Most citizens of Sabine, Harrison, and San Augustine Counties also took sides in these feuds. It is interesting to note that no constables were elected in these four counties during the republic.[17]

As debts rose to more than two million dollars, tariffs were the only real source of government funds in Texas. License and land fees, the poll tax, and other service fees also raised some money for the republic in its early days. Taxes on property were, for all practical purposes, completely uncollectable, and county government was funded largely by fees or fines of one kind or another. Constables and sheriffs were remunerated by service fees and travel allowances for service of various civil and criminal papers, attendance at trials, property appraisals, summoning juries, and other duties. During most of the republic, the several constables and the sheriff in any county, working closely with the justices of the peace, became very important as the primary sources of county government operating funds.

One exception to the overall organization of Texas counties was Bexar, which had only a town constable—no police or sheriff's department to keep the peace throughout the county. Because of the perpetual uncertainty of peaceful coexistence with Mexico, which mounted two brief invasions of the area later in 1842, San Antonio counted relatively few Anglo-Texans among its permanent residents, and only occasionally did a magistrate ride into town.

About this time a group of rangers was organized as a scouting detail of the Texas Army, to ensure early warning of Indian or Mexican forays into populated Texas. About forty of these rangers manned a small exposed fort on the frontier along the Brazos River, not far from where Marlin is today.[18]

A TROUBLED LAND: INDIANS AND INVASIONS

Politics at the republic level added to the problems of keeping the peace. Sam Houston could not succeed himself as president of the republic, so in December 1838, Mirabeau Buonaparte Lamar was elected to the office. Houston and Lamar were not good friends and held very different philosophies. Whereas Houston avoided further war with still hostile Mexico, attempted to keep peace with the American Indians, and worked for annexation by the United States, Lamar took just the opposite approach. President Lamar pursued policies that brought the Texas Army, the militia, and the newly organized ranging companies into a series of bloody campaigns against various Indian tribes and Mexico.[19]

Not a man of small gestures, President Lamar initiated his dealings with Mexico by offering five million dollars in exchange for recognition of Texas's independence. Though this offer was not accepted, Lamar was very successful in obtaining recognition of Texas sovereignty from other nations, including France, the Netherlands, Belgium, and Great Britain. In 1839, recognizing the size of the republic, Texas again moved its capital, this time to a frontier location on the north side of the Colorado River in Central Texas. The new city was named Austin.[20]

During the spring and summer of 1839, minor skirmishes with various Indian tribes took place, and Texans made a series of observations of "Mexican, Indian, and Negro peoples" traveling in Texas together. In March 1839, one such group was discovered and attacked by Colonel Edward Burleson of Bastrop about five miles east of present-day Seguin. In that fight some thirty Mexicans and Indians were killed, and nineteen were captured. In May of that same year another group of Mexican and Indian riders was discovered and attacked near a crossing on the North San Gabriel River. There the Texans captured 114 head of pack mules and horses, along with 300 pounds of powder, another 300 pounds of bar-lead, and incriminating correspondence between Mexican officials and Indian chiefs.[21]

Over the next several years, war with most Indian tribes in Texas took an ever-increasing toll in settlers' lives. In response, in 1839, recently migrated Cherokee tribes were forced to quit Texas and move north of the Red River. In early 1840, Comanches agreed to meet Texans for peace talks in San Antonio at the Council House. When the Comanches failed to surrender several white captives, a deadly fight broke out inside the building. The fight spread to the streets of San Antonio, and for the next several hours Comanches and Texans battled in what would be known as the "Council House Fight."[22]

Mirabeau Lamar, second president of the Republic of Texas (courtesy Western History Collections, University of Oklahoma Library).

After these battles, the Texans settled back to wait for more Indian attacks. They did not have long to wait. In August 1840, the Great Comanche Raid took place. What was to be the largest Indian raid ever in Texas took the settlers and the Texas Army by complete surprise. The first Texan encounter with the predominantly Comanche raiders was on August 5, 1840, near today's Hallettsville. Militia groups of several hundred armed Texans under captains Adam Zumwalt, Ben McCulloch, and John Tumlinson Jr. (son of Austin colony's first alcalde in the Colorado District) began to follow the trail of the raiding Indians.[23]

On August 6, numerous Comanches appeared outside of Victoria. They attacked the town, killed a number of settlers, and after capturing up to fifteen hundred head of horses and mules, retired a few miles north of town. By the evening of August 7, they had moved southeast toward the town of Linnville, located some three and a half miles north of what is today called Port Lavaca, on the banks of Lavaca Bay. Linnville citizens were also taken completely by surprise. No defense was possible, and the only escape was toward several boats in the bay, including the coastal steamer *Mustang*. Later on August 8, the Comanches began to burn the town of Linnville, and by nightfall left with several hundred horses and mules loaded with stolen goods.[24]

To the north, various militia groups organized and positioned themselves between the Comanches and the Texas Hill Country above where San Marcos is located today, and where the Indians had passed on their way south. By the morning of August 12, 1840, the two hundred militia men, including thirteen Tonkawa Indians, had reached Plum Creek and were prepared to fight the Comanches. On came the Indians—warriors as well as older men, women, and children, who had come on the raid to share in the loot. Among them were captive white women and children. With them also were two to three thousand horses and mules, many loaded with loot from Victoria, Linnville, and countless homes that were raided along the way.[25]

The Texan forces attacked the Comanches as they crossed the open plain, and then chased and killed them for another fifteen miles, to near where the towns of San Marcos and Kyle are located today. Whereas it is estimated that at least eighty Comanches were killed, only one Texan died and seven were wounded at the Battle of Plum Creek. The Comanche raid at Plum Creek was the first and only raid into Central Texas in which the Indians met a large body of

Ben McCulloch, Indian fighter and Confederate Army general (courtesy Texas State Library and Archives Commission).

armed Texans. It was also the last known major Indian raid sponsored by the Mexican government. Just two months later, in October 1840, more than four hundred Comanche and Kiowa warriors raided over four hundred miles into Mexico, killing everyone and everything in their path, including an estimated fourteen hundred Mexicans in the states of Nuevo León and Coahuila. It has long been speculated that the raid into Mexico, so soon after the Comanche defeat at Plum Creek was to pay back the Mexican government for not supporting the Comanches who took part in the Linnville raid.[26]

Eventually the Southern Comanche tribe was pushed out of the San Antonio region and north of the Colorado River. The remnants of the Cherokee and other Indian tribes principally in East Texas

Battle of Plum Creek, August 12, 1840 (courtesy Texas State Library and Archives Commission).

were chased to North Texas, into what would soon be called Indian Territory, north of the Red River. Although various Indian tribes continued to raid into Texas primarily from Mexico and the High Plains north of Texas, Lamar's Indian campaigns were effective and gave Texas several years of relative peace from major Indian depredations.

In December 1841, Sam Houston again took office as president of the republic. Mexico greeted the new Houston presidency with two invasions of Texas by the Mexican Army. The first (which was also the first invasion by Mexico since 1836) was discovered by Texas Ranger Captain Jack Hays, whose warning gave settlers in San Antonio a much needed few hours to escape before the Mexican Army arrived in March 1842. Led by General Rafael Vasquez, this incursion turned out to be nothing more than a brief plundering expedition. In a few days, the Mexican soldiers packed up and headed back toward the Rio Grande.[27]

The second invasion was not detected, and on the foggy morning of September 11, 1842, a thousand Mexican troops arrived in San Antonio, led by General Adrian Woll, a French soldier-of-fortune. Just nine days later, as armed militia and volunteer troops gathered near San Antonio, General Woll's army packed up, took a number of civilians prisoner, and retreated toward Mexico. It would be the last time Mexican Army troops would be on Texas soil until 1846, when Mexico would wage a war that would cost them almost one-third of their territory.[28]

During his last presidential term, Houston was preoccupied with negotiations between Texas representatives and the government of the United States. While the United States continued to balk at annexation, Britain and France acting as intermediaries between Texas and Mexico, supported the republic's continued independence in return for Mexico's recognition of Texas. Houston's second term as president came to an end, and Anson Jones became president of the republic in December 1844.[29]

THE REPUBLIC OF TEXAS IS NO MORE

President Anson Jones worked quietly for annexation by the United States. In February 1845, after the U.S. Congress passed resolutions offering annexation to Texas, Mexico indicated to English

John C. "Jack" Hays, captain in the Texas Rangers (courtesy Panhandle-Plains Historical Museum, Research Center, Canyon, Texas).

Anson Jones: "Texas Is No More." The last president of the Republic of Texas (courtesy Texas State Library and Archives Commission).

diplomats that they were now willing to recognize Texas's independence, if Texas would reject annexation. To the vast majority of Texans, the offer came ten years too late.

In June 1845, the Republic of Texas Congress met and approved annexation by a vote of fifty-five to one. A new constitution for the future state of Texas was drafted, and again the government provided for its county governments, including the election of constables. Article IV, Section 13, provided that "there shall be appointed for each county a convenient number of justices of the peace, one sheriff, one coroner, and a sufficient number of constables."[30]

On December 29, 1845, a year almost to the day after Jones's inauguration, Texas was officially annexed, becoming the twenty-eighth state of the United States, when the U.S. Congress accepted Texas's new state constitution. On February 16, 1846, the U.S. flag was raised over Austin, and Texas's last president, Anson Jones, declared, "The Republic of Texas is no more." Two months later, on April 23, 1846, Mexico declared war on the United States.[31]

For the next fifty years, Texans fought Indians, Mexicans, and each other, and died in rather large numbers for every foot of ground settled between the Colorado and the Rio Grande Rivers, and from the area north of the Brazos to the Red River.

CHAPTER IV
THE LONE STAR STATE, 1846 TO 1873

FROM ANNEXATION TO SECESSION

Within four months of the annexation of Texas, Mexican troops crossed the Rio Grande, and the United States and Mexico were at war. For almost ten years, Mexico had feared and forestalled (as best they could) Texas's absorption into the United States. Between the revolution and Texas's annexation, Mexico continued on occasion to mount armed invasions into the republic. But these so-called invasions amounted to no more than occasional harassment, with no land occupied for more than a few days or weeks, and they were of little consequence to anyone north of the Rio Grande, except, of course, to those few who were killed. By making no serious effort toward a lasting peace with the republic (which with some assistance from Europe at critical times, might have forestalled Texas's eventual union with the United States) Mexico had gambled foolishly. Several important Texas politicians would have preferred to see Texas remain independent.[1] Yet Mexico's decision to wage war over what it had lost ten years earlier resulted only in greater losses in lives and land—this time more than one-third of its territory.

In its first year, the Lone Star State launched thirty-one new counties and an economic boom that would last almost fifteen years. Suddenly Texas had access to money, an army, and more settlers to counterbalance the ever-occurring problems of living on the edge of civilization.

James P. Henderson was voted first governor of the state of Texas, and Houston and Thomas J. Rusk went to Washington, D.C., as the state's first U.S. senators. With few exceptions, county government under the 1845 Constitution differed little from that under the republic's constitution. The county board still comprised a chief justice and four county commissioners. The new office of

James Pinckney Henderson, first governor of the Lone Star State (courtesy Texas State Library and Archives Commission).

county treasurer was instituted, and tax assessor's duties were expanded. Two county offices, surveyor and treasurer were appointive, but after 1850, all county officials were elected for two-year terms.[2]

On May 12, 1846, the Texas Legislature passed an act "Defining the Office and Duties of Constables," which clearly outlines the peace-keeping or law-enforcement duties of a constable in the first years of the Lone Star State. A second act, passed that same month, outlined similar duties for sheriffs, who were given the additional duties of keeping the jail and guarding prisoners. The latter act also confirmed the authority of constables on the American frontier. It stated that the constable shall be the "conservator of the peace throughout the county, and it shall be his duty to suppress all riots, routs, affrays, fighting, and unlawful assemblies, and he shall keep the peace, and shall cause all offenders to be arrested, and taken before some justice of the peace."[3]

Though the population of Texas quadrupled during the years of the republic, by the census of 1850, the mostly rural population had jumped to 212,000. By 1860, on the eve of the Civil War, Texas had more than 600,000 citizens. In 1850, with just under five thousand residents, Galveston was the largest city in Texas, but by 1860 San Antonio had gained that distinction, with a population of 8,200. That same year the population of Houston was only about 4,800.[4]

Cotton was the engine that drove the Texas economy from 1845 to 1860. In 1848, some 40,000 bales of cotton were exported, but by 1860, approximately 420,000 bales had been shipped to mills on the east coast of the United States and in Europe. Rice and sugar beets were also major cash and export crops. Yet in only a few years, statehood had ensured sufficient security from Mexican and Indian raiding in the Texas brush country that cattle raising became Texas's second-most important industry.[5]

When Texas was annexed, a peculiar thing happened: instead of entering the union by treaty, and as a territory, Texas was admitted directly into the union as a state. As a result, the Texas state debt remained with the state, but so did all of its public domain. No other state was granted this concession. Texas was also admitted with more territory than the republic could control or legitimately claim. In addition to the land controlled by the Republic of Texas, the land ceded to the United States by the Treaty of Guadalupe Hidalgo, signed by Mexico in January 1848, included all of New Mexico, most of which was also claimed by Texas. The United States agreed that Texas could hold the area around El Paso but not the area of New Mexico that it had never controlled, establishing more or less the state boundary as it exists today.[6]

In general, after annexation, the Indian tribes living in and on the edges of Texas remained pacified or less hostile as U.S. Army troops moved into a series of new frontier forts in Texas and regularly

patrolled the frontier. Although smaller, more warlike bands continued to raid and kill isolated settlers, most were overwhelmed by the
sudden appearance of the larger, better trained, better armed, and
more aggressive military force.

As the state of Texas settled into a more peaceful and prosperous
period, the business of county government and law enforcement expanded. One of the major political and military figures of the Texas
revolution (and the man whose name was given to the seat of
Guadalupe County), Juan Nepomuceno Seguin, returned to Texas
after several years in Mexico on family business. In the 1850s,
Seguin served as a Bexar County constable. He later moved to
Wilson County, where he served as county judge.[7]

THE CIVIL WAR AND RECONSTRUCTION

In November 1860, Abraham Lincoln was elected sixteenth president of the United States, and on December 20, South Carolina
seceded from the Union. Throughout the southern United States,
secessionist factions took action to follow South Carolina into the
Confederate States of America.

In Texas, Sam Houston, who had become governor, was ada-
mantly opposed to secession, but the majority of the people and
most powerful politicians were not. Houston was ignored, and in
late January 1861, a Secessionist Convention in Austin voted to
leave the Union, and join the Confederate States. Houston refused
to take the oath to the Confederate States, and so was replaced as
governor by Edward Clark.[8]

On April 12, 1861, the Civil War began with the shelling and capture of Ft. Sumter, South Carolina. A new Texas Constitution was
drafted and ratified that year, but it contained no new provisions in
regard to existing county government. County government and law
enforcement in Texas were often in chaos from the beginning of the
Civil War in 1861 to the end of Reconstruction in 1873. From
1862 to 1865, many county government positions went begging
for candidates. Beginning with the election of 1862, constables, justices of the peace, surveyors, and coroners were seldom elected or
appointed in most counties. In many jurisdictions, other elective
and appointive offices were also vacant. This was because most of
the more qualified men left home to serve in the Confederate Army

Governor Sam Houston. Opposed to secession, Houston refused to take the oath to the Confederacy in 1861, and was replaced as governor (courtesy Western History Collections, University of Oklahoma Library).

and Navy, or left Texas for work in other areas both in the Confederacy and the Union.[9]

All types of law enforcement suffered. Although there was usually a county sheriff, those elected were usually older and less qualified than previous officers. In addition, the ranger organization's funding was cut after most of its officers joined the Confederate Army and for all practical purposes ceased to exist until after the war.[10]

Most Texans served in the Confederate forces on one of several fronts—in the Army of Northern Virginia, principally in the 4th Texas Infantry, referred to as "Hood's Brigade"; in Tennessee, primarily with the 8th Texas Cavalry or "Terry's Texas Rangers"; in New Mexico, or back home in Texas, along the Red River or the Texas Gulf Coast, usually in Galveston. Efforts to intercept or fight hostile Indian tribes now raiding more often into Texas were sporadic at best.

On April 9, 1865, almost four years to the day after the war had begun, the Army of Northern Virginia, which was the only significant army left to the Confederacy, surrendered at Appomattox. The Civil War was almost over, and Texas prepared itself for the arrival of Union troops of occupation. Lt. General Philip Sheridan was made Military Governor of Louisiana and Texas, and was determined to make a strong show of force in the Lone Star State. The army of occupation consisted of two Union cavalry divisions that came overland from Louisiana and three Union Army Corps that came mostly by ship to various ports along the Gulf Coast. On June 19, 1865, the Union Army occupied Galveston, making it their headquarters.[11]

In only six years, Texas had lived under several different constitutions and a host of differing laws, rules, and regulations. This turbulence had caused a tremendous upheaval in the justice system. From 1865 to 1873, the rule of civil law would be on leave in Texas—martial law reigned. It would take several decades thereafter to reestablish civil code and process, even partially, in much of the state.

By August 1865, a provisional government was established in Texas, with General A. J. Hamilton appointed provisional governor. From 1865 to 1869, more than one-third of the county offices were vacant. Some counties were left initially without elected peace officers of any type. Most state office appointments were made by General Edward Canby, head of the Fifth Military District. During this period, the military made about two hundred appointments to regular state or county offices. In Austin, McLennan, DeWitt, Navarro, and Fayette, and a few other counties there was a single constable appointed by General Canby, but many counties had no constables during this period.[12] It should be noted that a significant number of "appointed" officials never actually took office. Some refused to qualify; some were "too sick to take office." Still others resigned within a few months. It was not a popular government in which to serve.[13]

As hard as it may be to believe, Texas at the end of the Civil War became an even more violent land than during most of the war. Even though few major Civil War battles were fought in Texas, two factors increased the violence after 1865. The first was that thousands of slaves had been brought into Texas by owners who were attempting to escape the Union Army advance into other areas of the Confederacy from 1863 to 1865. These people were suddenly free, but without means of support or roots to cling to when the Union won the war. In addition, tens of thousands of Confederate Army veterans returned home to Texas in the first six months of 1865, many with no more than the clothes on their back. More than a few continued to use a gun to forge lucrative lives of crime. Occupation by a conquering Union Army caused as much destabilization in some areas of the state as it created stability in other areas.

In February 1866 a State Constitutional Convention was held in Austin; but with limited participation by the people in Texas. This constitution altered county government somewhat by lengthening the term of all county offices (except for treasurer) to four years and by creating the new office of county attorney, which was to be appointive by the county board. A few months later, J. W. Throckmorton was elected the first governor under this constitution.[14]

In August 1866, more appointments were made by the new constitutional government, but many vacancies remained. As with the 1865 appointments, many of the appointees never took office. According to state records, they left the county, resigned, died, were killed, failed to qualify, or failed to serve. Most of those who served did so until 1870, when the Constitution of 1869 took effect.[15]

County government under the 1866 Constitution lasted only about fourteen months, because the Reconstruction Acts of March and July 1867 imposed a military government over the civil government. Texas took on the status of a conquered province, under military rule. In July of that year, General Philip Sheridan removed the elected governor and replaced him with Military Governor E. M.

Pease, who was more to his liking. In addition, Sheridan removed Texas county government officials in many counties at will.

Besides manipulating civil and criminal administration within established counties, the Army by 1868 also began establishing a series of new frontier army posts. Thirteen new army posts, from Fort Richardson in the north to Fort Davis in the far west, and Ringgold Barracks in the south, gave the frontier new protection against hostile Indian raids.[16]

In 1869, the second Reconstruction Constitution—Texas's fifth constitution in almost thirty years—effected some significant changes in country government. The county governing body, formerly the county board, was now the early day commissioners court and comprised only judicial officers. Article V, Sections 19, and 20 of the constitution called for the election of five justices of the peace in each county. Any three of the five county justices of the peace constituted the court, with one always representing the justice of the peace from the county seat, whose job was to serve as presiding officer.[17]

Other major county officials were county clerk, treasurer, sheriff, surveyor, county attorney, and five constables. Article V, Section 21 of the 1869 Constitution, called for a constable to be appointed in each precinct by the justice of the peace on the county board. The offices of county judge, coroner, and tax assessor and collector were abolished. Several enacted changes fostered corruption: justices of the peace now assessed county taxes, and the sheriff was required to collect them. Justices were also required to appoint their own constables. This arrangement lasted past the end of Reconstruction and into 1873.[18]

Consequently, between 1869 and 1873, no constables were elected in any county in the state. Whether the prescribed number of constables were appointed in every Texas county isn't clear, but it seems unlikely. Few could have relished serving any government—military or civil—so unpopular with local citizenry. From 1871 to 1873, however, the Texas governor appointed a number of people constable in selected *towns*, including Bonham, Brenmond, Clarksville, Cleburne, Crockett, Henderson, Kaufman, La Grange, Linden, and Mount Pleasant.[19]

Despite state and county government provisions set forth in the Constitution of 1869 and Texas's readmission to the Union in March 1870, military and carpetbagger civil government clung to

Union Brigadier General Edward Canby, head of 5th Military District in Texas. Canby made many of the civil appointments to offices in Texas counties during occupation (courtesy Texas State Library and Archives Commission).

Union troops of occupation in Brownsville, Texas, 1867 (courtesy Texas State Library and Archives Commission).

power through voter fraud, appointment, and passage of laws favorable to themselves. In January 1870, Edmund J. Davis, a carpetbagger from Florida, was elected governor by suspiciously narrow margin. He served until 1873.[20]

The actual administration of state, districts, and counties in Texas from 1870 to 1873 was accomplished by keeping the chosen few in office and others out of office by the passage of laws extending the terms of those in office, and by giving the governor the power to appoint officials. Elections scheduled for 1871, therefore, were not held until November 1872.

To further ensure the rule by the Radical Republican faction, two bills passed by the Texas Legislature in 1870 increased law enforcement activities in the state significantly. The first was a bill authorizing the organization of twenty companies of rangers to guard the northern and western frontier. The second established the Texas State Police in July 1870. The adjutant general was made head of both the rangers and the state police. There were almost 250 officers and persons of other ranks authorized for the state police.[21]

The legislation gave the state police power to make every sheriff, constable, marshal, and city policeman a member of their forces on demand. The state police was formed primarily to assume the role of the army in protecting loyal Unionists from intimidation and coercion by former secessionists. Although the state police also sometimes acted to ensure law and order, that seemed to their many critics a secondary objective.[22] The vast majority of state police seemed to be appointed because of political affiliation rather than law-enforcement ability; a large number were freed slaves. Substantiating this perception during the first twelve months that the state police were active were a number of incidents, one of which involved constables in Nacogdoches County.

On December 14, 1871, Justice G. Dawson was holding court in the Lynn Flatt Precinct in Nacogdoches County, almost twenty miles from the county seat. Two state policemen, Columbus Hazlett and William Grayson, who lived nearby, attended the justice court session. Apparently in disagreement with some action by the court, they caused a disturbance and threatened to shoot one of the lawyers. Justice Dawson charged them with contempt, and the two then left the court. An arrest warrant was issued, and Dawson gave it to Constable John Birdwell to execute. Constable Birdwell summoned a man named David Harvell to assist him in the arrest of the

Edmund J. Davis, governor of Texas during Reconstruction, 1870–1873
(courtesy Western History Collections, University of Oklahoma Library).

two state policemen. The constable then located Officer Hazlett nearby and arrested him. Hazlett offered no resistance, and on Birdwell's command called to Officer Grayson in a nearby store.[23]

When Grayson drew near, Hazlett told him, "I am a prisoner." Officer Grayson said, "Die before you surrender." Deputized Constable David Harvell then demanded Officer Hazlett hand over his gun. Instead, Hazlett drew his weapon and shot Harvell in the chest. But Harvell did not go down. He staggered through a nearby store door, picked up a shotgun, and fired the first barrel into Hazlett's face. Hazlett was hit by only a few pellets, but the second barrel discharged in the direction of Grayson, wounding him. Hazlett and Grayson returned fire, twice hitting Deputized Constable Harvell, who dropped dead on the store floor. Constable Birdwell never had a chance to draw his weapon, and was looking down the barrels of the state policemen's guns when they mounted their horses and rode off toward Grayson's nearby home. There they called dozens of neighbors to their house and declared their immunity from arrest.

Nacogdoches Sheriff R. D. Orton and a posse of about fifteen men arrived in the community of Lynn Flat two days later looking for the killers. They did not find the two state policemen and returned to Nacogdoches. On December 19, Constable John Birdwell answered a knock on his door in Lynn Flat and was shot dead. Sheriff Orton and the posse returned, and all suspected Constable Birdwell had been shot by Hazlett and Grayson. Arrest warrants were issued for the two, but again they were not found.

About a week later Lieutenant Thomas Williams, a respected member of the state police rode into Lynn Flat with two prisoners, William Grayson and Columbus Hazlett. Lieutenant Williams negotiated with Sheriff Orton for several days over the arrest and confinement of the two policemen. No settlement was reached, and Williams rode away one night with his two prisoners. Soon after, the head of the state police, Adjutant General Davidson returned to surrender Hazlett and Grayson to Sheriff Orton.[24]

The first year of state police activity in Texas seems to have been the most violent, for both lawbreakers and law abiders. If state police were generally feared and hated by most Texans, the organization itself did little to enhance its public image. The chief of the state police, Adjutant General James Davidson disappeared in November 1872, along with over $34,000 of state money. It was learned later that Davidson had fled to Europe; he never returned to Texas.[25]

Owing to a Democratic majority in the Texas Legislature in 1873 and the resentment built up in the hearts and minds of many Texans during the first two years of its activities, the Texas State Police were deactivated in April 1873. Although they stood accused of many excesses and numerous criminal acts, they also arrested 581 people charged with murder in the two years and nine months that they were active.[26] Whether the Texas State Police desired or fully deserved their notoriety, it could not have been too surprising. The organization had been birthed primarily by partisan politics, for the express purpose of limiting the freedom of the vast majority of Texans, who to the victorious Union Army and its supporters seemed, after all, little more than traitors.

In evaluating the Texas State Police, it is perhaps worth looking at two of the most famous men associated with the organization. The first is legendary Texas Ranger Captain L. H. McNelly, who was for several years a captain in the state police. He was even wounded in Walker County when he and another state policeman attempted to arrest several alleged murderers of a black man near Huntsville. Somehow McNelly's reputation survived his service with the state police, and he became one of the most respected Texas Rangers after Reconstruction.[27]

The second is the infamous John Wesley Hardin, who killed more than two dozen men, yet is often excused as a product of the excesses of the state police. Hatred of the state police was so strong that sympathies were with Hardin when at age fifteen he killed two of them to escape capture after killing a black freedman. Unfortunately most forget that Hardin had, at age thirteen, already attacked and stabbed a schoolmate with a knife.[28]

Constables throughout Texas had an undeniable role in enforcing the law across much of the state before the Civil War. It was not until after that war, when more roads and railroads were built; communications including the telegraph improved both within and between frontier counties; and the need to jail more offenders became commonplace that the sheriff really became the most important law enforcement officer in most counties. Until the 1870s, constables were often the most active law enforcement officers in their precincts, and, therefore, in their counties.

L. H. McNelly, captain of the Texas State Police (1870–1873), and captain of the Texas Rangers (1874–1876) (courtesy Western History Collections, University of Oklahoma Library).

I suggest that much of the developing importance of the Western sheriff was the result of the turmoil that followed the Civil War. Most of the rural constables on the American frontier were largely inexperienced in handling the more violent offender. Constables also had few deputies to call on for assistance, had no holding facilities of their own for offenders, and were accustomed to dealing with lawbreakers who often were their neighbors. They were no match for the large group of poor, restless, gun-carrying former soldiers from both armies who began moving into the West.

These drifters had less regard for life and the law than those living in most communities before the Civil War. As a result, the role of the constable began to diminish. During this same period, many a sheriff also stepped back to allow the better paid, more experienced, and often more ruthless town marshal to dispense justice to most of the lawless drifters in his county.

But more was happening in Texas during the early 1870s than Reconstruction politics. Cattle ranches in Texas were suffering from the lack of manpower, an almost nonexistent market, and the after effects of neglect during the war. To alleviate their economic plight, in the spring of 1871, ranchers undertook the largest round up and cattle drive to that time. During that year, almost seven hundred thousand head of beef cattle were driven from Texas—mostly to Abilene and Newton, Kansas.[29]

In Kansas, state legislators had made county constables elective offices and town constables appointive offices. By 1872, perhaps to differentiate themselves more distinctly from county constables, town constables in Kansas adopted the title town marshal. By the time Texas cattle and cowboys arrived in the Kansas trail towns, such famous, or soon to be famous lawmen and onetime constables as "Wild Bill" Hickok, "Cap" Whitney, and Wyatt Earp were already enforcing the law.[30]

The railroads also began to lay new track after 1865. Just five years after the end of the Civil War, even though Texas had almost doubled the number of miles of track, it still amounted to only some seven hundred miles. Three years later, it had expanded to more than fifteen hundred miles of track. Over the next two decades, railroads in Texas would arrive in Dallas and Fort Worth, then proceed to El Paso and later to the Texas Panhandle, eventually reaching the state of Colorado. Other railroads would go from San Antonio to El

Texas trail herd en route to Kansas, 1871–1872 (courtesy Kansas State Historical Society).

Paso, and smaller lines would creep southward from Kansas into the Texas Panhandle.

Times were also changing for the Texas Rangers. Although ranger companies were organized in August 1870 to help protect the frontier, appropriations failed to fund many ranger activities, and by June 1871, the ranger companies were mustered out of service. As a result, responsibility for fighting hostile Indians on the frontier stayed with the U. S. Army.[31]

The Texas Legislature took their own action in dealing with the Indian problem. In late 1871, a new act of the Texas Legislature provided for twenty-four minute-men companies to be stationed in various frontier counties. Their activities closely resembled those of the prior ranger companies, but they were much more economical, and allegedly more effective.[32]

Reconstruction ended officially on November 10, 1871; but it was not until the U. S. General Amnesty Act of 1872 pardoned most former Confederate officials of various acts against the United States, including treason, that a more moderate group of politicians in Texas and the rest of the United States could break the power that various radical groups had held since the Civil War.

Chapter V
The Far West, 1874 to 1900

In 1873, state elections overthrew the radical element, and in 1874, moderates began replacing the many Reconstruction-era political appointees. In February 1876, Texas adopted the constitution that, with various amendments, stands today.

In writing the constitution of 1876, Texas legislators strove to bring more local control back into the individual Texas counties, and to reduce the role of appointed officials and centralized (state, district, or county) government. They took the justices of the peace out of the courthouse, declared that constables would be elected once more, and thereby again gave the settlement of minor disputes and the legal system back to the citizens at a precinct level. Today, some Texas politicians are again attempting to thwart local control by doing away with precinct, and even some county government offices.[1]

Richard Coke was the first governor elected after Reconstruction. Governor Coke had run on a law and order platform and soon began to follow through on his promises. On May 2, 1874, he commissioned John B. Jones as a major in the new Texas Ranger Frontier Battalion, which was to guard the frontier between the Red and the Nueces Rivers. Six companies of seventy-five men each were to make up this force.

Major Jones took personal command of the ranger activities on the western frontier, and Captain L. H. McNelly, formerly of the state police, commanded the special force of rangers on the Mexican border, west and south of the Nueces River. Despite their having been organized earlier as a quasimilitary organization, primarily in the capacity of irregular Texas and U. S. or Confederate Army troops, it was not until the 1870s that Texas Rangers acted for the first time as peace officers.[2]

Richard Coke, first governor of Texas after Reconstruction (courtesy Texas State Library and Archives Commission).

As Texans struggled to press far west into the the state, the Legislature passed an act on April 11, 1879, regarding appointment of county officials in unorganized counties. These were counties that had insufficient numbers of settlers and no desire to assume the costs and burden of organizing as a recognized Texas county, but nonetheless needed to conduct commerce and reduce lawlessness in their communities. This act recognized the appointment of notary publics, cattle and hide inspectors, justices of the peace, and constables by the commissioners court of counties to which the unorganized counties were attached for judicial purposes. The act again confirmed the state legislature's strong support of constables and their role in law enforcement.[3]

THE MEANEST TOWN IN TEXAS

Typical of El Paso's citizenry at the time of the Civil War were brothers Henry and John S. Gillett, wholesale merchants and men of some influence. Southern sympathizers, the Gillett brothers (apparently no relation to the later well-known Texas Ranger James B. Gillett) would feel the wrath of the antisecessionists as the South moved closer to Civil War. Both Gillett brothers left El Paso after the Union forces moved into the region. John S. Gillett came back to El Paso after the war and was elected constable in El Paso County Precinct No. 2 in 1878.[4]

At the end of the Civil War, El Paso had fewer than a hundred Anglo-Texans. Its ability to receive supplies and even mail was compromised by its isolation and the threat from hostile Indians. Even after civil government returned in 1866, El Paso remained a Radical Republican stronghold. For that reason, Collector of Customs W. W. Mills, a Lincoln appointee, was the most powerful man in the area.[5]

By early 1880, El Paso was still a town of less than five hundred people. There was no real law and order in or around the town, which was full of hard cases. And when Lieutenant George Baylor arrived in 1879 with his family and the first elements of the Ranger Frontier Battalion, he chose to set up headquarters not in El Paso, but in Ysleta, the county seat some fifteen miles to the southeast.[6]

The Ranger Frontier Battalion's first job was to chase and fight Indians. Controlling rustlers and other lawbreakers was their second priority. But as the railroad came closer and the population grew,

George W. Baylor, head of Texas Ranger Frontier Battalion in West Texas (courtesy Western History Collections, University of Oklahoma Library).

local law enforcement in El Paso broke down completely, as evidenced by the rapid succession of city marshals in a matter of months.[7]

In late 1880, El Paso City Marshal A. I. Stevens was fired after only a month in office, for "neglect and dereliction of duty." Stevens was replaced by a former Clay County Deputy Sheriff, George W. Campbell, who was sworn into office on December 1, 1880. City Marshal Campbell appears to have been an effective peace officer back in Clay County, and had been recommended to the city council by Ranger Captain George Baylor. But George Campbell left the job before January 1881 was half over. He was replaced by a new city marshal named Ed Copeland, who also lasted less than a month. The city marshal's position in El Paso appeared more a game of musical chairs than a serious attempt at law enforcement.[8]

About this time, the last significant Indian raid on the western frontier of Texas occurred when Apache warriors under Victorio attacked the San Antonio–El Paso stage coach in Quitman Canyon. Captain Baylor and his Texas Rangers trailed the Apaches into the Diablo Mountains, southwest of Guadalupe Peak, and attacked the group on January 29, 1881. The rangers killed four braves, two women, and one child before the Apaches fled north and finally out of Texas.[9]

Back in El Paso, the marshal's job continued to rotate. Ed Copeland was replaced by Deputy City Marshal Bill Johnson, who was more friendly with a whiskey bottle than he was with enforcing the law. Finally, in early 1881, the governor ordered the Texas Rangers to move to El Paso to assist the city marshal. During this period the Texas Rangers and a few constables tried to maintain law and order in El Paso.

Gus Krempkau had come to Far West Texas as a ranger with George Baylor in 1879. He later resigned from the Texas Rangers and moved to El Paso. The election records of November 2, 1880, do not show Krempkau was elected constable; apparently he was appointed to fill in for one who could not be bonded. Gus Krempkau took his work seriously. In early 1881, his work was mostly keeping the peace between groups of ranchers and their cowboys on both sides of the Rio Grande. These cattlemen often used a long rope to increase their own cattle herds.[10]

Before the railroad arrived in 1881, El Paso finally decided to solve its own law-and-order problems by recruiting a serious city marshal from outside the immediate area. On April 11, 1881, El Paso hired former Texas Ranger and Socorro, New Mexico, lawman Dallas Stoudenmire for the job. But trouble didn't wait for Stoudenmire's arrival. On April 12, Don Ynocente Ochoa, a respected large rancher and political figure in Mexico and a close friend of the rangers, approached Captain Baylor to complain about a loss of thirty head of cattle from his ranch in Mexico.[11]

He asked for help when the trail ran north across the Rio Grande to the John Hale Ranch outside of El Paso. Baylor would probably have been well advised to go himself, or to send several rangers, but he sent a single Texas Ranger, Private Ed Fitch, with the group of Mexican cowboys who had brought the request for assistance and could identify the missing steers. They had found only three head of cattle with Ochoa's brand on them at the Hale Ranch, when owner and sometime rustler John Hale, who claimed he had bought the cattle some days before, told them to get off his land. The ranger and most of the Mexican cowboys rode away, but two cowboys stayed behind to continue searching the underbrush for their cattle.

Two days later, on April 14, a larger group of armed Mexican riders again crossed the Rio Grande in search of the two Mexicans who had not returned. This time Constable Gus Krempkau was asked to accompany the group of riders going to the Hale Ranch. Krempkau spoke fluent Spanish and had proved himself an honest lawman on both sides of the border. Several other norteamericanos also rode along, including Ranger Fitch.[12]

Later that morning, the missing Mexican cowboys were found dead in the brush, apparently shot from ambush as they ate. While the bodies were taken to El Paso for inquest by Constable Krempkau, Ranger Fitch rode off to arrest rancher John Hale and two of Hale's cowboys who had been heard bragging about the killings. Fitch failed to nab his quarry, but Hale and two friends—Len Peterson and the recently fired City Marshal George Campbell—came to the inquest and argued that he and his men had not killed the Mexicans.

When the inquest was adjourned for lunch, most of those involved drifted off, including Dallas Stoudenmire, who had been appointed El Paso's new city marshal only three days before. Suddenly Constable Krempkau, who had been arguing to indict both of the self-confessed killers, found himself alone on El Paso Street with John Hale and George Campbell. Campbell, who had

Dallas Stoudenmire (standing), El Paso city marshal from April, 1881 to May, 1882; two others in photo not identified (courtesy Western History Collections, University of Oklahoma Library).

been drinking, yelled belligerently, "Any American that is a friend of Mexicans ought to be hanged!"[13]

Constable Krempkau challenged Campbell, saying, "George, I hope you don't mean me." Campbell shut his mouth, turned, and walked to his horse. Suddenly John Hale, who was partially hidden by Campbell's tied horse, pulled his gun. Coming up behind Campbell, he shot Constable Krempkau once in the chest. Krempkau slumped against a saloon door but had strength enough left to pull his own gun.

City Marshal Stoudenmire, who was eating lunch at the Globe Restaurant across the street when Krempkau was shot, came out of the restaurant running toward John Hale. He fired a quick shot at Hale, but hit and killed a bystander instead. Both Krempkau and Stoudenmire now shot at Hale. One bullet hit him in the head. Some observers say it was Krempkau's. Regardless, John Hale was the second to fall dead that day in the streets of El Paso.

Meanwhile, George Campbell had pulled his own gun, and Constable Krempkau, who was dying, shot again, hitting Campbell's gun hand. Campbell dropped his gun, but quickly scooped it up in the other hand, and Krempkau fired once more. But the constable was losing consciousness because of the deadly wound in his chest, and his poorly aimed shot managed only to hit Campbell in the foot. Stoudenmire then shot, at Campbell, hitting him in the body. Campbell dropped in the street and died the next day.[14]

Four men had been killed within seconds. One of them, Constable Krempkau, died because he had chosen to uphold the law and fight for equal justice. He was not the first Texas constable to die in line of duty, nor would he be the last.[15]

SOME CONSTABLES IN ACTION

The public record of constables and their deputies is both limited and scattered. To a large extent this is because most elected constables manned one-person offices, or at the most had one deputy. This arrangement has not changed greatly to this day in many counties, where patrol, criminal investigations, and the serving of papers are often lonely and dangerous. Both then and now, most constables' efforts have gone largely unheralded.

The local newspapers that publish stories about events in rural Texas were and often still are located in the county seat; many are published only weekly. As a result, they first record the activities of the sheriff or the town marshal, and later the police chief, whose offices were usually located just down the street from the newspaper office. Consequently, a constable's exploits in his precinct went mostly unreported and unheralded, except to those who lived in his precinct, or when a death was connected to an event. Nonetheless, the two following brief anecdotes survive to illustrate the diversity and range of constables' duties and activities during the late 1800s.

Shackelford County

In the 1870s, prostitution was at the center of many minor crimes. The *Fort Griffin Echo* reported on January 18, 1879, that two prostitutes had been engaged in a fight in Gus Huber's saloon. A constable arrested the pair and took them before Justice of the Peace Steel. One of the women immediately pleaded guilty and paid her fine. The other decided to argue her case with Justice Steel. He listened to her story, turned to the constable, and told him, "I believe this little girl was right," and directed her to be released.[16]

Lamar County

In February 1884, Constable W. D. "Bill" Nelson arrested John Middleton, cousin of notorious badman Jim Reed, for carrying a pistol and for three counts of bringing stolen horses into the state from Indian Territory.[17] In September 1884, Middleton escaped from the Lamar County jail, and in November of that same year he killed sheriff-elect Jim Black. A posse including Constable Nelson pursued but did not capture Middleton. Some time later Black's predecessor and his deputy were indicted and convicted of hiring Middleton to kill the sheriff-elect. In May 1885, John Middleton was discovered murdered in Indian Territory by a person or persons unknown.

TOO MUCH LAW AND NOT ENOUGH ORDER

Two days before his fifty-third birthday, the man who was to become one of the most famous constables in the state of Texas was elected to that office in Precinct No. 1 of El Paso County, which included the city of El Paso.[18] John Henry Selman ran as a Democrat in the election of November 8, 1892, against E. C. Jones, a

El Paso, Texas, in 1882 (courtesy Denver Public Library, Western History Collection).

The Overland Building, headquarters for the Texas Rangers in El Paso in 1881. George Campbell was taken here after he was shot by Stoudenmire and Krempkau (courtesy Border Heritage Center, El Paso Public Library).

Republican. Jones was better known than Selman in El Paso, and was expected to be the easy winner. But John Selman won by ninety-seven votes, taking fifty-three percent of the 1,503 votes cast.[19]

In the last decade, violence in El Paso had hardly decreased. City Marshal Stoudenmire, the only survivor of that 1881 gunfight that had left four dead (see page 64), had become a drunken embarrassment to the city fathers by the end of 1881. By March 1882, Stoudenmire was so often "sick" that the city appointed former Texas Ranger James B. Gillett as deputy city marshal. A month later, the still drinking Stoudenmire was found short of fines he had collected and resigned as El Paso's city marshal.

Like many out-of-work gunmen of the era, however, Dallas Stoudenmire bounced right back, and was appointed a deputy U.S. marshal for West Texas. He stayed in El Paso, only to be killed a few

El Paso City Marshal James B. Gillett (standing), appointed in 1882, after Dallas Stoudenmire was fired. Seated is L. S. Turnbo, an early day Texas Ranger and first sheriff in Pecos (courtesy Western History Collections, University of Oklahoma Library).

months later in a saloon gunfight. Despite the violence that plagued the city throughout the 1880s, El Paso grew from only about five hundred to more than ten thousand people, and became the county seat in 1883. In 1889, about a year after John Selman moved to El Paso, he was himself a victim of this violence. He was attacked one night, slashed by a knife about his face, and left for dead. Selman was apparently not the victim of a robbery. He appears to have been the victim of an assassination attempt, and later hinted as much. But Selman was lucky. In the dark, the knife had entered his mouth; blood gushed out, and the attackers probably thought they had cut his throat. They dumped him in a vacant lot and did not even rob him.[20]

Selman had moved to the El Paso area from New Mexico in 1888, and had worked for about the first year at the American Smelting & Refining Company. Two of his sons worked there briefly with him. For two years after the assassination attempt, Selman and his sons worked in a number of odd jobs, including driving large herds of cattle from the El Paso area to various parts of New Mexico. This kept him out of El Paso much of that time, which may have been what he wanted.[21]

Then in late 1892, he returned to El Paso to run for constable. There is no record of why John Selman decided to seek election in El Paso, but the assassination attempt must have made him realize how very vulnerable he was as a private citizen. Perhaps he thought he would better the odds of defending himself. As an elected peace officer he could wear a badge and carry a gun legally.

John Selman was no stranger to law enforcement or the violence that accompanied it by the time he was elected constable. He had once, briefly, been a deputy sheriff in Shackelford County and had been an active member of a bloody vigilante group, the Fort Griffin Vigilance Committee. In 1878 he saw John Larn, a good friend, former sheriff of Shackelford County and, many said, fellow cattle rustler, arrested and jailed in Albany, Texas. Larn was shot and killed by members of a vigilante group that took over the jail.[22]

Warrants had also been sworn out for Selman at the time Larn was arrested and killed, but he left Texas for New Mexico, becoming a participant in the bloody Lincoln County War. In 1880, Texas Rangers returned Selman to Shackelford County for trial, but local government released Selman, gave him a horse, and let him ride away. Some authors have called John Selman a rustler, murderer,

John Selman and his son John Jr. Photo likely taken in Fort Davis, Texas, during the late 1870s or early 1880s (courtesy R. G. McCubbin Collection).

John Selman as he looked about 1880, in Ft. Davis, Texas, when he was arrested by Texas Rangers and returned to Ft. Griffin, Texas (courtesy Western History Collections, University of Oklahoma Library).

and robber, and he was probably all of these, but he was never tried or convicted of any crime.[23]

Selman appears to have been dedicated to his sons. When he was elected constable in El Paso, the two adult sons who had been working with him for several years were still living near him. By that time, Selman had killed at least four men and probably closer to a dozen, yet it was not unusual to see him giving rides to children on his horse or them sitting on his lap as he told them stories. And when he died, "the whole town turned out to pay its respects at his funeral."[24]

We really know very few details of John Selman's life. This is somewhat unusual, because he was one of the last important gunmen in the Old West, before it became a more civilized land. Somehow, as an active gunfighter and an accomplished killer of men for more than twenty years, he had managed to live to the ripe old age of fifty-five years, at a time when life expectancy was less than forty-five. Although he was a contemporary of and more effective gunfighter than Clay Allison, Wyatt Earp, Bat Masterson, or Ben Thompson, Selman is still relatively unknown. This may be because Selman differed from many of the other gunfighters of his time. While many others sought reputation, fame, and sometimes fortune, John Henry Selman sought seclusion, disappearing altogether at various times during his life. It is said that he used one alias after another, but so did many others at the time, including a number of Texas Rangers and other lawmen. Selman was also quick to get out of town when things went wrong; perhaps that is what gave him the edge he needed to live another day.

In reviewing John Selman's life, it is quickly apparent to even the casual reader that he was like many other gunfighters—not always good, not always bad. The same could be said of many of the marshals, Texas Rangers, sheriffs, and other constables who helped tame Texas and the rest of the West in the late nineteenth and early twentieth centuries. John Selman was, in fact, like many another poor, uneducated westerner on the edge of civilization. He lived a hard and often dangerous life, and was generally good at whatever he chose to do—whether as a fugitive from the law or a peace officer in El Paso. He was also loyal to family and friends.

Much of what we can find about John Selman's life occurred in the few years he lived in El Paso, after he was elected constable. He began his new job on November 23, 1892, after posting a $1,500 bond. A few days after taking office, Constable Selman appointed

W. H. Wheat his first deputy. During his years in office, the court dockets indicate that Constable Selman was indeed busy, and was perhaps the hardest working law enforcement officer El Paso ever had.[25]

Selman and his deputy responded to complaints including disturbing the peace, burglary, swearing at an officer of the law, drunkenness, assault, theft, and adultery. In those days, fines were almost always preferred over giving the offender a jail sentence, and the average fine seems to have been five dollars. At the time, John Selman, "Uncle John" to some, was constable in Precinct No. 1, his twenty-year-old son, John Selman Jr., was an officer in the El Paso Police Department.[26]

In early April 1894, a deputy U.S. marshal and former Texas Ranger named Baz (often called "Bass") Outlaw came to El Paso as a witness in a trial. Baz Outlaw was what today would be called "a mean drunk." He was described by several who knew and liked him as his own worst enemy, and was considered unstable by many. In El Paso on April 5, Outlaw spent the early evening drinking at Tillie Howard's sporting house and making threats against his boss, U.S. Marshal Dick Ware of Alpine, for sending another deputy marshal to serve papers in his district. The more Outlaw drank, the more he cursed Ware.[27]

Outlaw left Tillie Howard's and walked up Utah Street, where he met Constable John Selman and Frank Collinson. Both men attempted to distract him from drinking too much, but he suddenly decided to go back to Howard's. Selman and Collinson went with him, hoping this would slow him down and take his thoughts off Marshal Ware. When they entered Tillie's parlor, Selman and Collinson sat down, but Baz Outlaw stepped out of the room.

Suddenly a gun went off in the house, and Selman got up and moved to the rear of the house to see what was going on. Tillie Howard ran through the room blowing a police whistle, as an alarm to trouble, and Outlaw ran after her. Others heard the whistle alarm, and Texas Ranger Joe McKidrict (whose real name was Joe Cooly) ran into the back yard, where he met Constable Selman, who told him, "It was an accident, Joe, he's all right." McKidrict saw Outlaw in the back yard, and demanded, "Bass, why did you shoot?"[28]

Baz Outlaw snarled, "You want some too," and shoved his gun against McKidrict's head and pulled the trigger. Ranger McKidrict

Texas Rangers, Company "D" at Realitas, Texas, in 1887. Baz Outlaw, who was killed by Constable John Selman in El Paso in 1894, is standing, second from left (courtesy Western History Collections, University of Oklahoma Library).

was dead before he hit the ground. Then, for good measure, Baz Outlaw stepped back and shot him again.[29]

Constable John Selman saw what happened, and as he stepped off the porch, he sensed what might come next and drew his gun. Outlaw turned, thrust his .45 in Selman's face, and pulled the trigger. As in the earlier assassination attempt, John Selman was lucky, for Outlaw's bullet just missed the side of his head, but the black powder in the fired round was driven into his face and eyes, blinding him. Selman's strong will to survive allowed him to fire a single shot at what he thought was Baz Outlaw's body. Outlaw received a fatal wound from "Old John's" only shot fired. Selman could now see almost nothing. Fortunately, the shot he had fired, which went through Outlaw's left lung just above his heart and emerged below his right shoulder, kept Outlaw from raising his gun high enough to kill Selman. It is a credit to Selman's professionalism as a peace officer and a gunman that he did not panic and empty his gun at any movement or shadow, which would have likely left several others dead or wounded that night.[30]

Baz Outlaw reeled back, managed barely to lift his arm, then shot twice at Selman, hitting him just above the right knee and in the thigh. As Selman went down, still not firing his gun blindly, Outlaw fell backward over the fence around Tillie Howard's sporting house and ran into Utah Street with a now empty gun, where he surrendered to a Texas Ranger and collapsed.

Baz Outlaw was dying; he expired approximately a quarter past nine that night in a prostitute's bed in the back room of Barnum Show Saloon. Constable Selman got himself into a carriage and went to see a Dr. White, who bound his wounds and confined him to bed immediately. As a result of his wounds, Selman would walk with the aid of a cane for the rest of his life, and his son, John Selman Jr., said his father was nearly blind at night from that time on.[31]

The district attorney required Constable Selman to stand trial for the shooting, on October 30, 1894, but asked for a directed verdict of acquittal. Judge Buckler agreed, as John Selman was not only protecting his own life, but was reacting to the murder of a fellow lawman by a drunken killer, who just happened to be a deputy U.S. marshal.[32] On November 6, 1894, just one week to the day after he stood trial for the killing of Baz Outlaw, the voters of Precinct No. 1 reelected John Selman to the position of constable in El Paso.[33]

John Selman Jr., city policeman in El Paso, 1890s (courtesy R. G. McCubbin Collection).

In addition to John Selman's reelection in Precinct No. 1, two other constables in El Paso County were reelected on November 6, 1894: Ben Blanchard in Precinct No. 2, around Ysleta; and J. A. Gilcrease in Precinct No. 5, which contains the community of Sierra Blanca in the southeastern portion of the county. New constables named Salgado and Benavides were elected, respectively, in Precinct No. 3, at Socorro, and Precinct No. 4, around San Elizario, along the Rio Grande River south of El Paso.[34]

JOHN WESLEY HARDIN COMES TO TOWN

In March 1895, ex-convict and newly qualified lawyer John Wesley Hardin arrived in El Paso. Hardin, one of the most notorious killers in North America, did not have to know or dislike a man to shoot him. He wrote in his autobiography that he had killed more than forty men. Others have said he killed somewhere between eleven and twenty-seven before being sent to prison in Huntsville, Texas, for more than fifteen years. In early 1894, he had been pardoned and released.[35]

Hardin began his infamous career in 1869, at the age of fifteen, when he shot and killed a black freedman in Polk County, Texas. It would be eight years before he was captured by bounty hunters and Texas Rangers on a train in Florida. According to his autobiography, in a single afternoon on a trail drive in Kansas, Hardin killed five Mexican cowboys, but what finally sent him to prison was the shooting of Deputy Sheriff Charles Webb of Brown County, Texas on May 26, 1874.[36]

But that was all behind Hardin when he arrived in El Paso. He had served his time, been pardoned, and picked up a new profession in state prison—he was now a lawyer. He did not have to wait long for work, because he was hired by Beulah Morose to represent her husband and recover a large amount of money, about three thousand dollars, taken from her by the Mexican police in Ciudad Juarez, Mexico. Beulah Morose was the wife of accused cattle thief Martin Morose (or M'Rose, or Morse, depending on the source) a Polish immigrant who had been recently arrested in Mexico, but not yet extradited to the United States.

It did not take long before John Wesley Hardin and Beulah Morose developed a relationship far more intimate than just lawyer and client. Beulah left her husband in Mexico and moved into the same boarding house with Hardin. Soon after, Martin Morose was released from jail in Mexico, but was not about to return to El Paso as long as he was a wanted man.[37]

By 1895, El Paso seemed populated by a number of aging gunmen. George Scarborough started his law-enforcement career as a constable in Jones County, Texas and became a Texas sheriff, and then a deputy U.S. marshal. Jeff Milton, former Texas Ranger, U.S. marshal, Texas sheriff, had become chief of police in El Paso. The El Paso County sheriff was F. B. Simmons. And traveling through, there were always a few others handy with a gun including an occasional New Mexico sheriff, like Charles C. Perry. Perry had bragged he would kill Hardin, and when John Wesley refused to fight him, had offered one of his two guns to a friend of Hardin's to provoke a gunfight. It never happened. But of some interest is the fact that Hardin's friend retained him to file assault charges against Sheriff Perry. Constable Selman, whose lot it was to arrest Perry, probably laughed as he took the New Mexico lawman to court.[38]

In Juarez, Martin Morose was anxious to see his wife Beulah, get some of their money that was now in her possession, and persuade her to leave Hardin and return to him in Mexico. Morose saw Deputy U.S. Marshal John Scarborough in Mexico several times, and mentioned his desire to slip into El Paso to see Beulah, but he was afraid to venture into the United States as a wanted man. Apparently Scarborough agreed to help Morose slip across a railroad bridge, where they were to meet after dark.[39]

As Morose walked across the bridge with Deputy U. S. Marshal Scarborough in the lead, two other lawmen shouted, "Hands up!" A few minutes later Morose was dead. Scarborough, along with Deputy U. S. Marshal Jeff Milton and Texas Ranger McMahan (brother-in-law to Scarborough) had shot Martin Morose almost a dozen times, after which, Scarborough claimed, Morose said, "Boys, you've killed me." Scarborough also says he told Martin Morose to "stop trying to get up, and we will quit shooting." The only problem with this alleged conversation is that a medical examination showed that two of the bullets that hit Morose went through his heart, killing him instantly.[40]

Morose's friends in Mexico cried out that John Wesley Hardin had the lawmen kill Martin to get the money from Beulah. Even the El Paso newspaper hinted some type of conspiracy, and the El Paso County Grand Jury indicted all three lawmen for the murder of

Martin Morose. But peace officers who killed outlaws (or each other for that matter) seldom went to jail in the Old West. The courts, and sympathy for those who carried and often used guns in Texas rarely censured the "winner" of such a fight. This case was no different. When it finally came up for trial, no witnesses answered the call and the case was dismissed.[41]

Constable John Selman's attitude toward Beulah Morose and John Wesley Hardin is not known. But about thirty days after Martin Morose's death, Policeman John Selman Jr. arrested Beulah for carrying two small .41-caliber pistols, and Hardin threatened Selman's son for the act. A few days later John Selman Jr., accompanied by several other policemen, arrested Hardin on a complaint from Beulah Morose. These events made neither John Selman nor John Jr. popular with Hardin. A few days after Hardin's arrest, Beulah left El Paso, taking a train to New Mexico.[42]

After his release, Hardin drank pretty hard and began doing dumb things over and over again, including robbing local card players. Hardin's petty robberies undoubtedly shocked and frightened his victims, especially when the most feared killer in Texas stuck a pistol in their faces. Initially, he got away with the robberies, but by mid-1895 people were standing up to Hardin and embarrassing him in plain view of the world. In May 1895, Hardin was arrested for unlawfully carrying a pistol and for the robbery of a card game. He paid a fine and when no one stepped forward to complain about the robbery, he walked away.[43]

Hardin apparently faced the problem by having another drink— and then another. He also lost at cards. To the casual observer, Hardin was a broken man, but Constable John Selman was no casual observer of killers—he was one himself. It must have weighed heavily on Selman that Hardin might revert to type at any time and kill someone. John Selman apparently decided that the someone was not going to be either his son or himself.

On Monday afternoon, August 19, 1895, John Selman stopped John Wesley Hardin on the street, and said he had heard Hardin had threatened John Jr. He then told Hardin to get his gun and settle the matter, but Hardin claimed to be unarmed. The *El Paso Daily Times* stated that at that point Hardin said, "I'll go get a gun and when I meet you, I'll meet you smoking and make you shit like a wolf all around the block." If Constable John Selman had been worried about his reputation as a gunfighter, he could have killed

Constable John Selman in uniform, El Paso Photo Studio (courtesy R. G. McCubbin Collection).

Hardin right there and claimed to believe that Hardin was armed. But Selman elected to walk away. He would, however, not be gone long.[44]

Some time after ten that evening, Hardin entered the Acme Saloon on San Antonio Street for a drink. As Hardin disappeared into the saloon, Selman approached the open front door of the Acme, and according to several witnesses hung around the entrance for some time. Some said John Selman entered the saloon at least once for a drink, and glowered at Hardin; others claimed he played a hand or two of cards with Hardin that night, but that seems unlikely.[45]

All we really know is that at about 11:00 P.M. John Selman stepped through the door of the Acme Saloon and shot John Wesley Hardin in the head. As Hardin fell to the floor, Selman apparently stepped over to Hardin and shot at him twice more (as was often done in gunfights of the time), hitting him once in the chest and once in the arm. One of his three bullets also shot off the tip of Hardin's left little finger, probably the result of Hardin throwing his hand up in defense before the first shot was fired.

Reflecting public opinion, the August 21 *El Paso Daily Times* ran the following: "The people of El Paso breathed a sigh of relief yesterday morning when they read in the Times the story of the killing of John Wesley Hardin at the Acme [on] Sunday [it was actually Monday] night by John Selman. Some said it looked like murder, but all agreed that it was what they had been expecting. Three out of four persons met said . . . Selman had done the proper thing in killing Hardin and taking no chances, while the fourth would admit that Hardin's death was a good thing for El Paso."[46]

In September, John Selman was indicted by the El Paso Grand Jury for the murder of John Wesley Hardin, and in February 1896, the trial began. Selman never claimed that he did not shoot and kill Hardin. It appears that his lawyers were most concerned about his claim that he shot Hardin as he looked at him—in the eye. There was a bullet hole just over the left eye of John Wesley; however, much of the evidence pointed to the possibility that Hardin was shot in the back of the head. The evidence for either possibility was conflicting, and the outcome of the trial was a hung jury. The *El Paso Times* of February 12 stated that the jury was split—ten for acquittal and two for conviction. Another trial was scheduled.[47]

In the weeks after the trial, John Selman's son accompanied him wherever he went, especially at night. Their main concern was a

John Wesley Hardin (courtesy Western History Collections, University of Oklahoma Library).

San Antonio Street in El Paso. This photo is believed to have been taken about 1885. The Wigwam Saloon was built a few years later, on the vacant lot on the right side of the street (courtesy Denver Public Library, Western History Department).

Gem saloon interior. John Wesley Hardin robbed the card games in the Gem Saloon several times (courtesy Border Heritage Center, El Paso Public Library).

killer, Mannie Clements. Mannie was a cousin of John Wesley Hardin, and had shown up in El Paso a few months earlier, after ambushing a man in Alpine, Texas. Mannie would later be a member of the El Paso Police Department.[48]

In spring 1896, John Selman was shocked when John Jr. was arrested in Juarez, Mexico, for the "abduction" of his fifteen-year-old sweetheart. The abduction was not forced. After no one in Juarez would marry the young girl to John Selman Jr., they had decided to slip off to a hotel, where they were discovered. The girl's family charged him with abduction. On April 4, 1896, Constable Selman visited his son in the Juarez jail, promising to return with Deputy U.S. Marshal George Scarborough to gain his release.[49]

But Constable Selman would never come back: the next night, April 5, he was shot in the back, and then three more times, by Scarborough himself, in the alley behind the Wigwam Saloon. Selman died the next day.

Jeff Milton and George Scarborough, deputy U.S. marshals and two of the killers of Martin Morose (courtesy Western History Collections, University of Oklahoma Library).

Arrested for the murder, Scarborough agreed five days later to resign from the Marshal's Service. In June 1896, he was tried for the murder of John Selman. He claimed he shot Selman in self-defense, and as usual in such cases, he was found not guilty. He soon left town, traveling to New Mexico, where he was employed as a detective by a group of cattle raisers. On April 6, 1900, four years to the day that John Selman died of his wounds, his killer George Scarborough died of a gunshot wound he received chasing train robbers in New Mexico.[50]

WHAT HAPPENED BETWEEN SELMAN AND HARDIN?

The events that actually took place in the Acme Saloon on the evening of August 19, 1895, have long been the subject of speculation and controversy. Though we know that Constable John Selman shot and killed John Wesley Hardin, we do not know why or exactly how.

Gunfight in an El Paso street. Although this gunfight took place after 1900, El Paso could still be called "the meanest town in Texas" (courtesy Border Heritage Center, El Paso Public Library).

The Wigwam Saloon became the Wigwam Theater, shown here. Scarborough killed John Selman in the alley near the exit door (courtesy Border Heritage Center, El Paso Public Library).

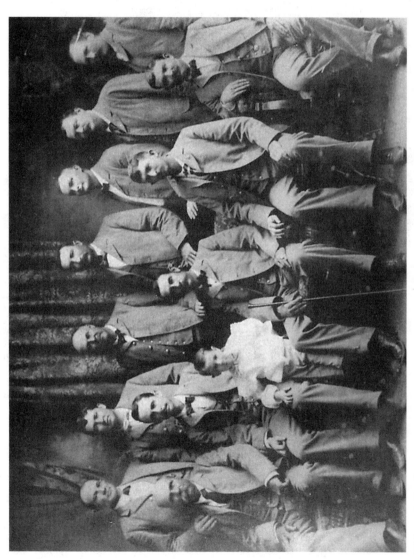

El Paso Police Department in 1887. Mannie Clements, seated second from right, was a cousin of John Wesley Hardin, and thought by Selman family to be a potential assassin. He was said to have been a constable, but there is no record of his election in El Paso County (courtesy Border Heritage Center, El Paso Public Library).

The respected author Leon Metz, in his book *John Selman Gunfighter,* published in 1966, presented two versions of why Selman killed John Wesley Hardin. In his later book *John Wesley Hardin: Dark Angel of Texas,* published in 1996, Metz proposed three possible reasons, or a combination thereof, as possible motives for the shooting: jealousy of Hardin, the Morose money, or an insult or threat by Hardin to himself or his son.[51]

Nothing recorded seems to indicate that Selman had an ego that fed on bragging and publicity, which is the very opposite of John Wesley Hardin. Nor is there anything that would seem to bear out jealousy as a credible motive for Selman's killing Hardin or anyone else. Nor does Selman appear to have been given to enlarging his reputation in Shackelford County, New Mexico, or El Paso. Hardly anything is known of the four or five people Selman is credited with shooting before Baz Outlaw. The stories of those killings are largely incomplete, and even the full names of most of those shot are not certain.[52]

In regard to the "Morose money," no one who participated in or testified regarding Morose's demise claimed that Selman was in any way involved. Speculation that Selman was associated with the Morose murder appears unfounded. Selman was not reported present at the shooting. He was not prosecuted by the grand jury, nor was his name even brought up during the trial of the admitted killers. The Morose murder appears to have been a Scarborough family affair.[53]

Selman's defense in court was that Hardin had insulted him and his son. To Selman, an insult from John Wesley Hardin was tantamount to a death threat, certainly an arguable position. We know that Hardin most likely held a grudge against John Jr. for the arrest of Beulah Morose, and later for his own arrest. We also have statements from Selman and others that Hardin threatened Old John himself. What better way to thwart a killer, than to kill him first?

But John Selman may have had another significant motive for killing John Wesley Hardin—his appreciable loss of vision as a result of the shot Baz Outlaw fired toward his face a few months earlier. John Selman Jr. confirmed that his father could no longer see at night. Night blindness, or a general loss of sight, was not something Constable John Selman was likely to talk about, given that he had to patrol at night. It is not unreasonable to suspect that this newfound vulnerability combined with Hardin's direct or implied threats may have left John Selman looking for any opportunity or an excuse to kill Hardin.[54]

With regard to the question as to how John Selman shot Hardin, either in the back or facing him in the eye, there is evidence for both scenarios. It is not overly surprising that alleged eyewitness accounts gave both versions. In the best of situations, eyewitnesses often contradict each other. The admitted killer, John Selman, says that as he passed behind Hardin, he saw Hardin's eye in the mirror, saw movement he assumed was Hardin drawing his pistol, then drew his own gun and shot Hardin before Hardin could shoot him. Selman claims he shot him in the face because of his fear that Hardin was wearing the fabled iron breastplate. Three examining doctors testified that the entry wound was in the back of the head.[55]

But a photo of the dead John Wesley Hardin lying on his back shows a small neat hole just over the left eye—not a typical exit wound for a .45-caliber revolver. Unfortunately the back of the head was not photographed, but the photographer, a man of some experience, said that the wound over the eye looked like no other exit wound he had ever photographed, and he believed that Hardin had been shot from the front. It should also be expected that John Wesley Hardin, if he had been shot in the back of the head, would have been thrown forward and would have fallen on his face; in fact, after Hardin was shot, he was flat on his back.[56]

We will never really know exactly what happened. No speculation can now resolve these inconsistencies. We do know, however, that John Selman was not afraid to stand face to face with death, as he had done with Baz Outlaw only a few months earlier. We also know that John Selman treasured his two sons.

For good reasons, Selman was very wary of John Wesley Hardin. Selman had confronted Hardin earlier in the day, and could have killed the then unarmed man easily. We know that others, including lawman and bounty hunter Jack Duncan, who actually captured Hardin in Florida and sent him to prison in Texas for more than a decade, considered Hardin still to be very dangerous.

In an interview, Duncan said he learned that John Wesley Hardin had threatened "to come to Dallas and kill him during the State Fair next October." Duncan then went on to say that he would have known about Hardin's coming to kill him before he "got on the train at El Paso," but that it "shows that John Wesley Hardin was at

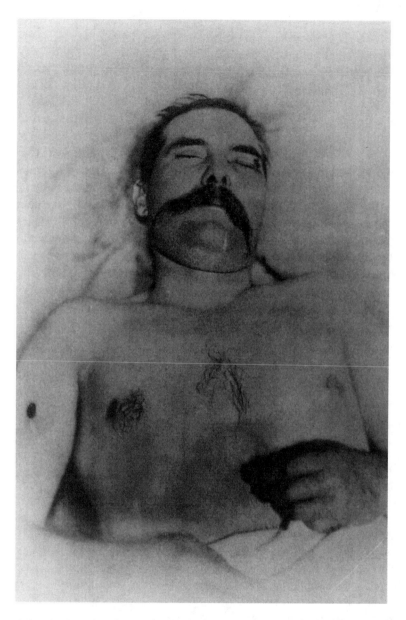

John Wesley Hardin, death photo. Note bullet wounds in Hardin's right arm, above left eye, and finger shot off on left hand. The small bullet hole above left eye does not appear to be an "exit" wound, and the "defensive" wound in left hand convinces some people, including the author, that Hardin was most likely shot while facing John Selman (courtesy Western History Collections, University of Oklahoma Library).

heart equally as much a bad man in 1895 as he was in 1875." John Selman would hardly have disagreed.[57]

Selman seemed to have been a pretty active lawman since his election three years earlier; at least that is what the El Paso newspapers of the day and most of the voters in his precinct said. Selman was now fifty-five years old, in an era when the average farmer and storekeeper lived no longer than forty-five years. He was crippled and walked with a cane. He was also nearly blind at night, and in a job in which vulnerability could easily mean death. Selman seems at least to have had more to fear from Hardin than George Scarborough did from Selman a few months later in that dark alley in El Paso. Apparently his boss, U.S. Marshal Dick Ware, believed so, for Scarborough was forced to resign, and he left Texas soon after. He would never again wear a deputy U.S. marshal's badge, but instead finish his law-enforcement career as a private detective for a cattlemen's association.

SOME OTHER WEST TEXAS CONSTABLES

As the nineteenth century came to a close in Texas, other constables were also busy. The following brief accounts exemplify the activities of Texas constables in the 1890s.

Johnson County

On November 2, 1897, John B. "Stokes" Shaw murdered a Johnson County ranch foreman in a jealous rage because of his desire for the foreman's wife. Shaw was arrested, tried, and convicted. In August 1898, Shaw broke out of the Johnson County jail just two days before he was scheduled to hang. Stokes Shaw was chased by posses from Johnson, Hill, Navarro, and Henderson Counties for almost two weeks without success. He was finally captured south of Malakoff, Texas, by Constable Walter Anthony of Henderson County.[58]

Williamson County

The first arrest of King Fisher, a notorious outlaw who was later elected sheriff of Uvalde County, was by Constable Ike Barber. Fisher was being transported by Barber to Georgetown when he

Deputy U.S. Marshal George Scarborough, killer of Constable John Selman in 1896. Although not convicted, he resigned as deputy marshal and left Texas (courtesy Western History Collections, University of Oklahoma Library).

broke free and escaped, never to return to the area again. Fisher was later killed along with Ben Thompson in San Antonio in 1884.[59]

San Augustine County

On April 21, 1900, Texas Sheriff George Wall was shot in the back with a shotgun by longtime enemy Curg Border. This murder of a lawman escalated a rivalry into a full-fledged family feud between the Border and Wall families. Both families were well-known early settlers in San Augustine County and prominent in politics.

Deputy Noel Roberts was appointed Sheriff and arrested Curg Border, who was quickly released on bond. A month later Eugene Wall, brother to Sheriff Wall, shot Ben Broocks, a close friend of the Border family, four times in the back, and refused to surrender to the sheriff after he reached home. Deeply troubled by the incident, Sheriff Roberts consulted with respected San Augustine County Constable John Matthews. Constable Matthews telegraphed the governor asking for a company of Texas Rangers. The next day Constable Matthews and Judge Tom C. Davis met and sent a second request to the governor, that a company of the state militia be sent to San Augustine to keep the peace, as local law enforcement was not thought capable of handling the situation.[60]

CHAPTER VI
THE TEXAS PANHANDLE,
1874 TO 1900

BUFFALO HUNTERS AND EARLY SETTLEMENTS

Exploitation and limited colonization of the Texas Panhandle began during the early 1870s, as professional hunters moved into the area to harvest tens of thousands of buffalo. In early 1874, Adobe Walls, a trading post, saloon, and campsite for those hunters was built on the north side of the Canadian River in what is now Hutchinson County.

The Indians on the Southern Plains were aware of the dangers to their way of life brought on by the slaughter of the buffalo. As a result, war parties from the Comanche, Kiowa, Cheyenne, and Arapaho tribes met in the Panhandle at a War Council in June 1874. They decided to stop the killing of the buffalo by killing the buffalo hunters. Their vendetta began on the morning of June 27, with an attack on Adobe Walls.[1] Estimates are that up to seven hundred Indians attacked twenty-eight hunters and traders there, but they failed to take the post and lost as many as eighty men in the effort. This defeat did not stop the Indian attacks on isolated hunting parties, however, and over the next few weeks a dozen buffalo hunters were killed.[2]

The U.S. Army reacted to the Indian attacks, and from August 1874 to June 1875 a punitive expedition consisting of five columns of combined cavalry and infantry attacked the Indian war parties in what is known as the Red River War. Fourteen pitched battles occurred in the Texas Panhandle, ending Indian domination of the Southern Great Plains.[3]

Despite the many battles fought in the Panhandle, estimates are that more than six million buffalo were killed on the Great Plains in 1874. In subsequent years the slaughter of buffalo continued, with an estimated ten million killed per year by the mid-1870s. In 1875,

Buffalo hides in Dodge City. Scene at Rath and Wright's yard in the 1870s (Courtesy Kansas State Historical Society).

Bones of thousands of buffalo on Great Plains in 1875. The bones were also a "crop," as they were collected and sold (courtesy Western History Collections, University of Oklahoma Library).

buffalo hunters established a major camp along Sweetwater Creek for resupply and to sell their hides. They called the camp Hidetown, locating it in what would become Wheeler County, near the army post of Fort Elliott. Hidetown grew rapidly as more hunters and skinners arrived. Within a few years, Hidetown, rough as it was, had become the first real town in the Panhandle, complete with saloons, restaurants, dance halls, freight yards, and a few homes for the people who worked there.[4]

With prosperity came the desire to abandon the name Hidetown, and adopt something better suited to what the local merchants hoped would develop into a main commercial center of the Texas Panhandle. Sweetwater was their first choice, but another Texas community had already used the name. So the Indian name Mobeetie, meaning "sweet water" was chosen for what has been called the "Mother City of the Panhandle."[5]

RANCHERS, RUSTLERS, AND RAILROADS

Along with the buffalo hunters and the townspeople of Mobeetie, two pathfinders also moved into the Panhandle in 1875 and 1876. The first of these pathfinders was Casimiro Romero, who had listened to the wonderful stories of older sheepherders who had been to the South Plains. He and his family moved the first large herd of sheep from the Sangre de Cristo Mountains of New Mexico to the north side of the Canadian River. They established the town of Old Tascosa, which became the second permanent settlement in the Panhandle.[6] The second pathfinder was not interested in sheep, but in cattle. He was a former Texas Ranger living in Colorado, and his name was Charles Goodnight.

Once the Indians were out of the way, Charles Goodnight drove his cattle out of Colorado, south past the Canadian River to Palo Duro Canyon. His idea was to find an area protected from the harsh, cold winds during the winter, with good grass and water, an area that would not need a strong fence, but where the high walls of the canyon would keep his cattle penned in. In 1876, Goodnight established the huge JA Ranch, the first permanent ranch in the Panhandle.[7]

The Texas State government recognized that with the hostile Indian tribes leaving the High Plains, it was only a matter of time until settlers would arrive, and the need for local government would require the organization of county governments. So on May 18, 1876, the region was subdivided into fifty-four counties and placed under the temporary jurisdiction of Clay County, in north central Texas. At the time, land in the Panhandle was controlled by railroads and the state land trust for schools.[8]

To organize a county, all that was then necessary was for the local citizens to present a petition signed by at least 150 qualified voters, hold elections, and designate a county seat. In 1878, Wheeler County qualified as the first county in the Panhandle to be so organized. At that point, fourteen other unorganized counties were attached to Wheeler County for judicial assistance.[9]

The first election held in Wheeler County took place on November 5, 1878. Michael Welsh was elected constable in Precinct No. 1 and Hugh McKay in Precinct No. 5, the only two precincts that elected constables. To no one's surprise, Mobeetie was named the county seat. Because Wheeler County voters elected many inexperienced county officials, justice, law, and order were slow in coming to Mobeetie, which remained a rough and fairly wild frontier town.[10]

Farther west, around Old Tascosa, organization of a county was still almost two years away in late 1878, when a number of those escaping New Mexico's Lincoln County War came to the town. Among them was Henry McCarty, better known as Billy the Kid. This group came with more than 120 horses—most suspected stolen in New Mexico—that they sold to area ranchers. All in Billy the Kid's group behaved themselves while in Old Tascosa. In fact, several men, including Henry Newton Brown, John Middleton, and Fred Waite left the Kid's gang. Brown stayed near Tascosa as an LX Ranch cowboy. Billy and the others rode back to New Mexico with some cattle stolen from nearby Texas ranches.[11]

By 1881, a railroad had been built across Texas to El Paso and beyond, and other railroads were being planned and built. During the 1880s, a number of counties organized throughout the Panhandle, and new cattle ranches staked out vast grazing areas for herds that numbered up to twenty thousand head.[12] Rustling became a major problem for the ranches along the Canadian River. In 1880, Bill Moore, owner of the LX Ranch, was concerned enough to hire Frank Stewart to represent his interests in New Mexico.[13]

On November 22, 1880, the Canadian River Cattlemen's Association, later called the Panhandle Stock Association of Texas, sent a contingent to New Mexico in an effort to stop Billy the Kid and his

Laying railway track near Canyon, Texas. Railroads largely dictated the settlement and economy of the Texas Panhandle after 1890 (courtesy Panhandle-Plains Historical Museum, Research Center, Canyon, Texas).

Two passenger trains collide on December 7, 1908. Three people were killed and several injured in this wreck between Amarillo and Canyon, Texas (courtesy Panhandle-Plains Historical Museum, Research Center, Canyon, Texas).

Three Lincoln County, New Mexico, sheriffs, 1877–1881: Pat Garrett, seated at left; John W. Poe, a former constable in Shackelford County, Texas, in 1878, seated at right; and James Brent, standing (courtesy Western History Collections, University of Oklahoma Library).

Henry Newton Brown was indicted for the murder of New Mexico Sheriff William Brady during the Lincoln County War; came to Texas with Billy the Kid, stayed on, and became a respected deputy constable in Oldham County. He was later city marshal in Caldwell, Kansas, and was captured after a failed bank robbery in Medicine Lodge (courtesy Kansas State Historical Society).

gang from rustling any more Texas cattle. Included in the group were Charlie Siringo, Jim East, Lon Chambers, Lee Smith, and C. W. Polk from the LX Ranch; Monroe Harris, Tom Emory, Louis or Lewis Bousman, Bob Roberson, and Billy McKoley from the LIT; and Bob Williams, Frank Clifford, and "Uncle Jimmie" from the Littlefield Ranch.[14] Upon their arrival in New Mexico, the cattlemen's association representatives met with Sheriff Pat Garrett of Lincoln County, who was also after the Kid's gang. Garrett chose four of the group from Texas and three of his own posse to go after Billy the Kid. Within a few days, after a hard and smart pursuit, the gang was surrounded and surrendered to the posse, who placed them in jail. Billy the Kid was found guilty of murder and sentenced to death. Just fifteen days before his hanging, he killed two guards and escaped the Lincoln County jail, forcing Pat Garrett to pursue him once again.

John W. Poe, who had taken Frank Stewart's place as an agent of the Panhandle Stock Association of Texas in Lincoln County, New Mexico, received the tip that sealed the Kid's fate. This was the same John W. Poe who had been overpowered as a deputy sheriff at Fort Griffin, Texas, in 1877, and whose prisoner, former Sheriff John Larn, was taken by a mob and killed. Poe was later elected constable in Precinct No. 4 in Shackelford County in 1878. He would succeed Pat Garrett as sheriff of Lincoln County, New Mexico, and had served two years as a deputy in Wheeler County, Texas, but lost the election for sheriff by one vote when gambling interests solidified against him.[15]

Poe contacted Garrett and tried to convince him that an informant swore that Billy the Kid was returning to Fort Sumner. Garrett was skeptical, but deputized Poe, who then accompanied Garrett and his deputy, Thomas McKinney, to Fort Sumner to make sure Billy the Kid did not return to the Texas Panhandle to steal more Texas cattle. Poe was right, and Garrett finally killed the Kid in the dark bedroom of a ranch house on the outskirts of Fort Sumner on July 14, 1881.[16]

In the U.S. census of 1880, there were only 1,607 people counted in the Texas Panhandle, but more than 108,000 sheep and 97,236 head of cattle. By 1886, the Panhandle Stock Association of Texas represented owners of almost three hundred thousand head of cattle. To manage those herds, ranchers began stringing barbed wire. The fences would keep their cattle in and strays and unwanted

Henry Newton Brown was caught robbing the bank in Medicine Lodge, Kansas. Caldwell, Kansas, City Marshal Brown (wearing neckerchief), his deputy Ben Wheeler (tall man on right), William Smith, and John Wesley (next to them) stand captured, after killing two bank officials in failed bank robbery. Brown was killed when a lynch mob came after them that night. The three others were hanged without trial (courtesy Kansas State Historical Society).

Outside the Equity Bar in Old Tascosa (courtesy Panhandle-Plains Historical Museum, Research Center, Canyon, Texas).

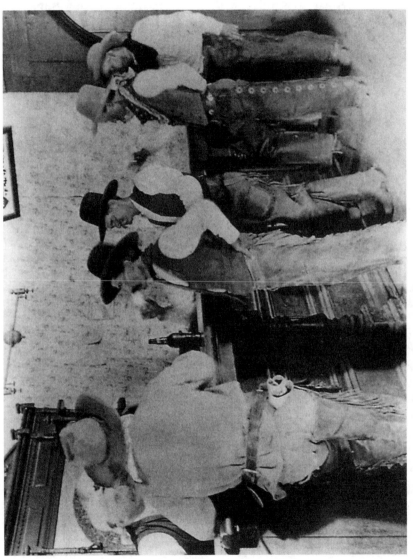

Inside the Equity Bar in Old Tascosa: left to right, Bartender Jack Cooper, Charlie Meyers, Marcello Sandoval, Henry Lyman, Bert Killion, and Marion (Mel) Armstrong, the first constable elected in Oldham County (courtesy Panhandle-Plains Historical Museum, Research Center, Canyon, Texas).

livestock, especially sheep, out. It would also keep diseased cattle from drifting into the area from north and south of the Panhandle.[17]

During this time Old Tascosa, located just northwest of where the city of Amarillo is today, was rapidly becoming an important settlement in the Texas Panhandle. It was the main trading town for a number of large ranches—the LIT, LX, LE, LS, and the Frying Pan. By late 1880, the area around Old Tascosa was booming, and on December 8 of that year, Oldham County was officially organized, with what locally was called Upper Tascosa becoming the first county seat.[18] Elected on January 12, 1881, as the county's first government were James E. McMasters, county judge; C. B. Vivian, county clerk; Marion Armstrong, constable in Precinct No. 1; and Cape Willingham, sheriff. The Willingham and Armstrong families had lived in the Panhandle for several years and were very close. Marion and Cape served on the mail route from Tascosa to Dodge City when Oldham County was organized.[19] Oldham was a county organized by citizens of Tascosa, who elected their neighbors and friends in and around the town. Because of its location and the maturity of those elected, the law-enforcement and court sectors in Oldham County grew in importance over the next several years. The unorganized counties of Castro, Dallam, Deaf Smith, Hartley, Moore, Potter, Randall, Sherman, and Swisher were attached to Oldham County for law enforcement and judicial purposes.

In its early years, Tascosa had been a relatively peaceful community as it grew to a population of almost six hundred people. But in 1881, some of the lawless element who had left Mobeetie began to show up in Tascosa. Most worked for one of the cattle ranches around Tascosa. In 1881, violence finally came to Tascosa when Frank (or Fred, as he has been sometimes called) Leigh was shot and killed by Sheriff Cape Willingham.[20]

When Leigh arrived with the first cattle herd brought to the LS ranch in the spring of 1881, Tascosa, like many other towns in the West, had an ordinance banning firearms. In June, he and several other cowboys rode away from Tascosa very drunk and ran into Constable Marion Armstrong and his deputy constable, Henry Newton Brown (who had come to Tascosa with Billy the Kid two years before and was also an occasional cowboy for the LIT Ranch). Brown and Armstrong were walking south of town looking for several horses that had drifted away from their pasture.[21]

Prominent citizens from Oldham County, Texas, 1884. Standing, left to right, are Surveyor W. S. Mabry, merchant Frank James, County Clerk C. B. Vivian, and attorney I. P. Ryland; seated (left to right) are Sheriff Jim East, County Judge James McMasters, and Pat Garrett, captain of the Panhandle Stock Association of Texas's "Home Rangers" (courtesy Western History Collections, University of Oklahoma Library).

Railing against the ordinance, Leigh proceeded to curse the town and its officials, and challenged Brown and Armstrong. But the two Tascosa officials were not about to go up against a half dozen of the LS Ranch cowboys' guns and returned to town in an agitated state. They soon met Sheriff Cape Willingham and others who had had run-ins with Leigh and the LS cowboys. They all agreed to watch for trouble and signal each other for help if it became necessary.

Only a few hours later, Leigh, who was still drunk, and several of his friends came back into Tascosa to do more drinking. As they rode into town, Leigh drew his revolver and shot at several ducks along the side of the road, killing one. This caused a great commotion, and one young woman screamed and fainted. Sheriff Willingham, Constable Armstrong, and another man, who were behind a nearby store, came running to the street at the sound of gunfire. Willingham stopped Leigh and others and demanded their guns. All refused, because neither Armstrong nor the sheriff were wearing their own guns at the time.[22]

Leigh and the other LS Ranch cowboys rode off toward the saloon. Cape Willingham sent Armstrong and the third man for backup, while he went to the rear of the saloon, where he'd left his sawed-off shotgun. Approaching the saloon, Leigh was cocky, as he had successfully bluffed the local lawmen twice that day and still had his guns. As Leigh dismounted, Sheriff Willingham came around the corner of the saloon, raised his shotgun and called to Leigh to surrender his gun.[23]

Leigh did not turn around, but vaulted back into his saddle and began to pull his own gun. Buckshot from both barrels of Sheriff Willingham's weapon hit Leigh in the body and blew him out of the saddle. Leigh's friends saw Constable Armstrong, Deputy Constable Brown, and several other townspeople all armed and moving toward the saloon and quickly rode off. Marion Armstrong held an inquest on the spot, clearing Willingham of any wrongful action.

Constable Brown went on to carve himself quite a reputation. He not only served with pride as a lawman in Texas and Kansas, but became a killer in New Mexico and a bank robber in Kansas. As the story goes, Brown was a hard man by anyone's standards. While serving as deputy constable in Tascosa, he had disarmed and brought to court a cowboy who after too many drinks had fired several shots from his pistol in the air. The cowboy told the court that Tascosa was nothing more than a bunch of adobe huts, and they had no right

Texas Panhandle cowboys, 1885 (courtesy Western History Collections, University of Oklahoma Library).

to bring him to court. Brown apparently took great offense at the comments and slammed his gun on the table between himself and the cowboy. Taking two steps back, he challenged the cowboy to try for the gun. The cowboy refused to take the dare, paid his fine, and in disgrace rode out of town as quickly as possible.[24]

In the 1882 elections, Sheriff Cape Willingham was barely defeated by an LX Ranch cowboy, Jim East. East had been with the posse headed by Pat Garrett that had gone after Billy the Kid several years before. Cape Willingham, of course, had already proven himself to local citizens by keeping the peace in Oldham County, but had become very unpopular with the growing population of cowboys after he shot Frank Leigh.

On the east side of the Panhandle, Wheeler County and the town of Mobeetie were finally finding their way forward. In 1881, aggressive prosecution of offenders by District Attorney J. N. Browning and stiff sentencing by Judge Frank Willis saw the decline of lawlessness in Mobeetie. The November 1882 election installed Sheriff G. W. Arrington and Constables Joseph Mason in Precinct No. 1, J. Aslip in Precinct No. 2, and Will Sanders in Precinct No. 4. Over the next several years, better law enforcement drove out the last of the really bad men in Mobeetie.[25]

Having more or less dispensed with the outlaw element, large landowners turned their attention to other concerns. In 1884, the big ranchers in the Panhandle hired Pat Garrett to form a group called the Home Rangers, which made its headquarters on the LS Ranch in Oldham County. Ostensibly, the group was to protect Panhandle ranchers from cattle thieves, but in practice it often devoted itself to isolating and driving out smaller ranchers and homesteaders. Texas Governor Jim Hogg gave the rangers credibility by authorizing their police powers. [26]

Large ranches controlled most of the land and money, were the largest or often the only employers, and had legitimized chasing suspected cattle rustlers across state lines by private posse. In the isolated Texas Panhandle, the owners of many larger ranches, particularly those along the western border, established considerable political clout by loaning Panhandle communities and county governments money to build courthouses, jails, and other improvements. In turn, the grateful communities housed grand juries that granted the Home Rangers power to harass small ranchers and farmers, whom large landowners deemed undesirable. As Panhandle

G. W. (Cap) Arrington, sheriff of Wheeler County and former Texas Ranger captain who, beginning in 1881 with newly elected court officials in Wheeler County, brought an end to the wild days of Mobeetie (courtesy Panhandle-Plains Historical Museum, Research Center, Canyon, Texas).

Wheeler and Oldham County officials in 1887. Standing, left to right, Deputy Sheriff Joe Mason and Sheriff G. W. Arrington of Wheeler County; Cape Willingham, first sheriff of Oldham County. Wheeler County officials seated left to right, District Clerk N. F. Locke, County Judge Emanuel Dubbs, and Treasurer J. J. Long (courtesy Panhandle-Plains Historical Museum, Research Center, Canyon, Texas).

counties organized in the late 1870s and throughout the 1880s, larger ranch owners sponsored their own cowboys and others sympathetic to their cause as candidates for local political office. Jim East's election as sheriff in 1882 exemplifies the ranchers' clout, as does the election in that same year of Louis Bous[m?]ar, who replaced Marion Armstrong as constable of Precinct No. 1. East was in turn succeeded in 1887 by Tobe Robinson, a former LS Ranch range foreman. In 1890, Robinson became Hartley County's first sheriff. These men were brave and effective lawmen, but sometimes owed too much allegiance to the larger ranches that helped elect them to office.[27]

During the early 1870s and into the 1880s, supplies came to the Texas Panhandle not from Fort Worth or El Paso, but from Dodge City, Kansas, or Las Vegas, New Mexico, by wagon train. By 1887, however, unorganized Potter County, which was attached to Oldham County and dominated by the large ranches, promised to be a major railhead for cattle trade in the decades to come. As the Fort Worth and Denver City Railroad reached northwest into Potter County and the site of what would become Amarillo, it became obvious that where it met and crossed other railroads heading into the Panhandle would become a vital commercial and trading center. Consequently, great efforts were invested by different groups to determine both the location of the county seat and its government.

Oldham County officials ordered organizing elections for Potter County to be held in August 1887. These elections would select the first county officials and the location of the county seat. Potter County had four precincts, but only Precinct No. 3 (controlled by the Frying Pan Ranch) and Precinct No. 4 (controlled by the LX Ranch) were inhabited by qualified voters.

Given the interests and influence of owners of these big ranches, it would be naïve to believe that Oldham County Sheriff Tobe Robinson, a former LS Ranch range foreman, had no agenda when he hired a twenty-one-year-old LX Ranch cowboy named Jim Gober as his deputy in July 1887. Nor could his appointing Gober to work in thinly populated Potter County only a few weeks before its first election of sheriff have been anything but an obvious effort to influence the vote.[28]

Three locations were in competition for the county seat, having met the criteria for eligibility. All three were on the railroad right-of-way, had ample water, and were far enough west in Potter County that a road built south toward Lubbock County would not have to circumvent the upper reaches of Palo Duro Canyon. On the ballot, the prospective county seats were named Odessa, Oneida, and Plains City, and their respective developers or owners engaged in considerable electioneering.[29]

Most of the qualified voters in Potter County lived and worked on the LX Ranch. J. T. Berry, the Oneida townsite developer, influenced John Hollicut, manager of the LX Ranch, to support his townsite by offering a free residence lot and a business lot to each LX cowboy who voted for Oneida. It was no surprise that in the August 6 election, Oneida won hands down—by forty-five out of fifty-three total votes, with Precinct No. 4 casting thirty-eight of the forty-five.[30]

In the August 30, 1887, election for county officials, all of the candidates favored by Precinct No. 4 voters were elected, including Jim Gober, who received twenty-one of the thirty-six votes cast for sheriff–tax collector in Precinct 4. Within the precinct, J. J. Sealey received all thirty-eight votes cast for county commissioner, and Elijah Lynch was elected constable with nineteen votes. Precinct No. 3 elected a county commissioner and Constable M. Beaver, and gave Jim Gober thirteen of the fourteen votes cast for sheriff–tax collector (combining the offices of sheriff and tax collector may have worked in some newly organized counties, but did not last long in most of Texas).[31]

The aggressive electioneering turned out a disappointing total of only fifty-one voters to decide Potter County's first officials, far fewer than in most county organizing elections, and it does seem curious that the other qualified voters in the county did not vote on their first election day.

Oneida, J. T. Berry's Section No. 188, was awarded the official townsite by the State Land Office in September 1887, but was soon renamed Amarillo. But another important group of land developers and many newly elected Potter County officials were not happy with section 188 as the site of the county seat. Throughout what was left of 1887 and into 1888, H. E. Sanborn, one of the owners of the Frying Pan Ranch, boasted he would spend $100,000 to move Amarillo. By trading for lots in Old Town and paying to move families a mile east, he convinced several county commissioners to transfer their homes and businesses to his townsite. He also donated a

Judge W. B. Plemons, first county judge in Potter County, and father-in-law of Sheriff Jim Gober (courtesy Panhandle-Plains Historical Museum, Research Center, Canyon, Texas).

large plot of land to the Union Church, and began construction of a forty-room hotel on his townsite.[32]

Another county election took place on November 6, 1888, to select commissioners and unfilled constable positions in Precinct Nos. 1 and 2 and various other Potter County officials, including justice of the peace, district attorney, and district judges. Jim Gober and County Judge W. B. Plemons, Gober's new father-in-law, were both reelected. M. M. Givins was elected the first constable in Precinct No. 1 by forty-seven of the fifty-seven votes cast. Billie Bell and G. L. Browning tied for the position of constable in Precinct No. 2, and Cal Walker was elected constable in Precinct No. 3.[33]

JIM GOBER SHOT ME

The ongoing townsite competition became old news in Potter County on Tuesday, January 10, 1889, when Sheriff Gober shot and mortally wounded Constable Givins in an Amarillo saloon. Early on January 10, Constable Givins received from the court three arrest warrants. The warrants were for Tom Cook, J. E. Shallcross, and William Taylor, all local citizens charged with illegal gambling. It was the second run-in with the law for Shallcross. That afternoon, Givins went looking for the three men and found two of them with several other people in the back room of L. B. Collins's saloon in Amarillo. Givins served his warrants to Cook and Shallcross, who according to eyewitnesses were protesting their arrest when two more customers, Thomas Arlington and Jeff Davis, entered the room.[34]

Constable Givens gave Cook and Shallcross the option to avoid court by paying their fines on the spot, a practice that was not unusual. Shallcross told Givins he had no money to pay the fine, and Givins replied that he would give him a day or two to raise the money. Cook argued with Givins, refusing to pay. For reasons of their own, the saloon owner, L. B. Collins, and Davis and Arlington began to kid and ridicule Constable Givins, accusing him of allowing other shady characters to walk the streets. The constable was not amused and complained about how he was being treated for doing his job. Angrily, he announced that it was his duty to serve the warrants, which had indeed been served.[35]

Collins, whose vested interest was obviously in his customers, asked who filed the complaint. Givins replied that it was none of his business and that the warrants had been issued by the court. Givins became more agitated as Collins continued to complain. When the constable approached Collins and said, "If you don't shut up I'll have every saloon man and gambler in town pulled [arrested]," Collins silenced and walked away.[36]

Givins had lost his temper foolishly and was apparently still mad. He paced up and down for a few minutes, then relaxed somewhat, and leaned back against a table. About this time three more men entered the back room of the saloon, John Hollicutt, the LX Ranch manager; Sheriff James Gober; and B. Hawley Plemons, the oldest son of the county judge.[37]

Constable Givins calmed down in the presence of another law enforcement officer, probably assuming that he could expect the sheriff's support in carrying out his duties. Givins now told Cook and Shallcross that he would not accept the payment of fines, that they would have to give the magistrate a bond and settle the cases before a judge, in court. Jeff Davis and another man then offered to go Tom Cook's bond, while the entire group, now apparently including Hollicutt and Gober, began to taunt Givins for serving the warrants. That one of his tormentors was another on-duty peace officer may have contributed substantially to Givins's revived anger. Givins was perhaps too inexperienced to understand that the reaction his warrants elicited was more reflective of the pervasive attitude toward the new statutory laws against gambling, intoxication, prostitution, and other vices (which were generally ignored throughout the Panhandle) than anything personal. Just the year before, a widespread disregard for such laws in nearby Crosby County had led to the so-called Bloody Grand Jury's returning thirty indictments on local citizens for these same offenses.

Regardless, it was Givins's misfortune that he now put a hand on his gun and said, "If you have anything against me, you better quit your monkey business, or turn your dogs off." It is interesting to speculate whether Givins was addressing the men he had just served warrants or Hollicut and Sheriff Gober. By *dogs,* he must surely have been referring to the group hazing him for doing his duty.[38]

Jeff Davis then said, "If I have said anything you don't like, if you will lay off your gun, I will whip you on half the ground you stand on." He then pulled off his coat, threw it on the table, and moved toward Givins.[39]

As a peace officer on duty, Constable Givins was in a precarious position. He had served arrest warrants on two men who were not cooperating and now was being threatened physically. Moreover, instead of lending the constable assistance, the elected sheriff of the county and several important citizens appeared to be party to the resistance. If Givins backed away, which the law clearly stated he was not required to do, his ability to enforce the law in that frontier community was over. On his deathbed, Givins wrote that Jeff Davis then "started toward me he being a larger man than myself I stept back and drew my six shooter." According to eyewitnesses, Givins did pull his gun slowly out of his holster and cover Davis and the group of men who were taunting him.[40]

At that juncture, Sheriff Gober held up his hand and sternly ordered Constable Givins to "hold up," but said nothing to Davis.[41] Although no one saw Sheriff Gober draw his gun, Givins wrote in his deathbed, "Jim Gober shot me." Gober himself admitted pulling his gun and aiming at Givins, but said the pistol went off without his knowing it.[42]

Givins received a mortal wound to the chest, and chose not to return fire, but dropped to the ground. Apparently Gober then went over to Givins and helped him to the hotel, where he was put to bed and attended by Doctor E. A. Jones. Constable Givins seems to have never lost consciousness, but acknowledged to several people that he had received his "death wound." Givins died two days later, and on January 14, after indictment by the grand jury, District Attorney W. H. Woodman filed charges against Jim Gober for Givins's murder. Gober was arrested, but released on bond until trial. Jacob Lowmiller, a former candidate for sheriff, was appointed to replace Constable Givins in Precinct No. 1.[43]

In mid-summer 1889, Gober began having problems with those who guaranteed his bond as sheriff and tax collector. One of his bondsmen, developer J. T. Berry, died, and a second bondsman withdrew support. On the same day the murder trial began, September 9, 1889, county commissioners met and declared the bonds of several elected officials, including Sheriff Gober, insolvent.[44]

The 47th Judicial District was formed in Potter County about the time Givins was killed, and L. G. Wilson was district attorney when the trial began September 9. Gober was acquitted two days later. This was no surprise, for all through the Old West, lawmen who killed outlaws or each other seldom if ever were convicted of committing any crime. If there was real guilt, the trial could be delayed a few years, at which point remarkably few witnesses showed up.[45]

The "Bloody Grand Jury," Crosby County, the grand jury that returned thirty indictments of local citizens for offenses ranging from gambling to prostitution to intoxication, as well as other vices generally ignored at the time by law enforcement and the courts (courtesy Panhandle-Plains Historical Museum, Research Center, Canyon, Texas).

Although he was acquitted, many believed Jim Gober should have gone to prison for killing Givins. It also seems that many Potter County officials did not want an accused murderer as sheriff and tax collector, regardless of how the trial came out. On October 7, four new bonds were approved for several county officials, but not for Gober or Jim Bain, county treasurer. They were allowed until October 10 to file new bonds, but Gober's and Bain's bonds were again rejected. Two days later, the offices of county treasurer and sheriff-tax collector were declared vacant by the court.[46]

On October 14, 1889, the commissioners court met to fill the vacant office of sheriff. Gober, A. F. Criswell, and J. P. Flores went before the court to apply. Criswell received three of the five votes and was appointed to finish serving Gober's term, which ended December 31, 1889. Jim Gober was never again to occupy the office of sheriff in Potter County. Gober was said to own an interest in and apparently ran a saloon in the bowery of Amarillo for a short time, but moved on to Oklahoma within a few months.[47]

WATER AND FARMING: A NEW PANHANDLE

As Amarillo grew and other railroads came to the Panhandle, it was not too long before Tascosa began to lose population. It appears that many who did not work for one of the larger ranches in Oldham and Hartley Counties thought there were better opportunities in a town like Amarillo. Mobeetie, the other longtime settlement in the Panhandle, also lost popularity, and after a few years both of these older communities were virtually abandoned.

There was a marked shift in the economy of the Texas Panhandle during the 1890s. Between 1890 and 1900, population in the Panhandle more than doubled; more than twenty-one thousand settlers were recorded in the 1900 census. In addition, between 1887 and 1902, twenty-three new counties were organized in the Panhandle, and local officials were elected. The Texas Legislature changed the future of the Panhandle in 1895 when it passed the Four Sections Act, which strongly promoted stock farming over open-range cattle ranching.[48]

During the next hundred years, the economy of the Texas Panhandle would be tied to intensive, deep-well, irrigation farming and cattle raising, not cattle ranching. Limited water supply, climate and weather patterns and the proportion of land dedicated to agriculture ensured that very few counties in the Panhandle would have population centers that could be considered large in comparison with many in Texas to the east of the High Plains. The total population of most Panhandle counties would remain much lower per square mile than most counties in the rest of Texas.

These factors have made local precinct offices such as constables and justices of the peace much less important as well as less likely to be funded than in areas of larger population, where higher rates of crime and large numbers of transients are found.

Lubbock, Potter, Gray, and Hockley Counties—the population centers of the High Plains—are the exceptions, and all have a larger number of constables and justices of the peace. Other counties in the area normally have a single county constable, and some no constable at all, although this means that the sheriff's department must employ extra deputies to assume the constable's workload. In this situation in many sheriff's departments, the service of civil process takes a back seat to most other duties.

CHAPTER VII
REFORM AND HARD WORK, 1900 TO 1946

A NEW CENTURY BEGINS

The transition from the end of the nineteenth to the beginning of the twentieth century was important to the American psyche. By the late 1890s, the Indian menace was gone and the American West was rapidly being tamed. Except in Alaska, expansion in the United States was mostly over. If Manifest Destiny were to continue, politicians and adventurers would have to look abroad for expansion of the power of the United States.

The Spanish-American War in 1898 was in many ways a watershed. For the first time since the Civil War, southerners, some of them former Confederate Army officers, supported U.S. forces, even joining volunteer regiments in that war against Spain. Cuba was freed, and in 1901 became a U.S. Protectorate. In the Philippines, war broke out between the occupying Americans and the rebel movement led by Aguinaldo.

The first two decades of the twentieth century have been described as an era of political, social, and economic reform. During this period, the United States adopted laws regulating business, broke up monopolies, expanded education, granted women the right to vote, and popularized populist politics.[1]

In Texas during the early 1900s, the missions of police, sheriff, and constable offices changed. The new mission of the Texas Rangers after 1900 exemplifies those changes. The last Indian battle was fought in Texas in 1881, in the Devil's Mountains of the Far West. But this did not mean the end of the Ranger Frontier Battalion, which wasn't abolished until 1901, when the state attorney general ruled that noncommissioned officers and privates in the Frontier Battalion had no right to serve papers and make arrests.[2] The Texas Rangers were then reorganized. They were officially named the Texas State Rangers from 1902 to 1934, when they became part of the Department of Public Safety. The Rangers in the first part of the twentieth century were suddenly a state police force, performing the same duties as, and often in competition with, local law enforcement. The Rangers' reputation suffered in the first years after reorganization, but their good and efficient work in the boomtowns and along the border quickly restored citizens' confidence.[3]

TINKERING WITH THE CONSTITUTION

By 1900, all but ten of the 254 counties in Texas had been organized. The Texas Constitution, then and now, served as the basis for county government. The governing body in the county is the commissioners court, composed of a county judge (sometimes a county judge at law), and normally four commissioners, each representing one of the county government precincts. In addition, a county clerk, tax assessor and collector, a county attorney, a sheriff, a county treasurer, several justices of the peace, and several constables are all elected to office.[4]

Differences between counties are based mostly on population, but also on a host of individual county initiatives that have altered the way county government is done. For example, in the early 1900s in counties with populations of more than ten thousand, the sheriff was no longer also the tax collector (except in San Saba County, where the sheriff was also truant officer and municipal police chief in 1970). In counties with eight thousand or more people, a district clerk was then and is now elected in addition to the county clerk, but in a few counties the same person still does both jobs.[5]

If there are more than three thousand school students in a county, a superintendent of schools can be elected, whereas in counties with fewer students, the county judge is normally ex-officio county school superintendent. Several county officials are even today appointed by the commissioners court, including a county auditor and county health officer. The county surveyor's office is now almost always left vacant. Constables and justices of the peace are elected in each precinct in most counties, but in a few counties for which a constitutional amendment has been passed, there may be only one constable or justice of the peace per county. As a result, there were and are differences between many Texas counties, and also between the precinct offices within counties.[6]

Bastrop County

Constables in Texas in the early 1900s were as likely to commit serious blunders as any other law-enforcement officer, and when violence created desperate situations, mistakes became more likely, and more deadly.

J. Virgil Dunbar was elected constable in 1906 in Precinct No. 8, then located in northeast Bastrop County. In August 1908, he and Dock McDavid went to the home of Joe McNeil to arrest him for public use of "abusive language." On the way to jail, McNeil jumped out of the buggy to escape, and McDavid jumped after him. McNeil grabbed for McDavid's gun. Dunbar fired three times at McNeil, but hit McDavid first and killed him; then he shot McNeil twice, killing him instantly. Dunbar was later indicted and tried, but found not guilty of murder.[7]

Cooke County

In 1907, one of Texas's most noteworthy law-enforcement careers began in Gainesville when Thomas R. Hickman was appointed deputy constable. Hickman had another job, with the Miller Brothers "101 Wild West Show." Hickman remained a deputy constable until 1911, when he was appointed deputy sheriff in the same county. Little is known about Hickman's work as either a deputy constable or deputy sheriff in Cooke County, although he remained a deputy sheriff for almost eight years. On June 16, 1919, Hickman was appointed a private in Company B of the Texas State Rangers by Governor William P. Hobby.[8]

After only two years in the Texas Rangers, Hickman was promoted to captain, and by 1935 to senior captain, but he soon resigned that office because of a dispute with Governor James V. Allred over the reorganization of the Texas Rangers into the Department of Public Safety. He joined the Gulf Oil Company Security Department not long after.[9]

While he was a Texas Ranger, Hickman worked at bringing law and order to a number of boomtowns in North Texas. He was also involved with capturing several notable bank robbers. Tall and good looking, he became a Texas celebrity in 1924, when he was judge at the first American Rodeo held in England. In the 1950s, he toured Europe with the Cowboy Band of Simmons (now Hardin-

Texas Ranger Captain Tom Hickman, Jim Jones, and Adjutant General W. W. Sterling (courtesy Western History Collections, University of Oklahoma Library).

Simmons) University as the official representative of Texas. In 1957, Hickman was appointed to the Public Safety Commission, which governed the Texas Department of Public Safety. He held that post until 1961, when he became chairman of the Commission. He died just one year later.[10]

Bell County

Bell County in Central Texas is the home of Mary Hardin Baylor College, still well known today. In the early twentieth century, Belton, the county seat and home of the college, contained a number of boarding houses where young ladies lived during the school terms. In July 1910, the summer term was in session.[11] Just after 1:00 A.M. on July 22, Constable James W. Mitchell of Precinct No. 1 received a telephone call from Dr. L. T. Batte, a teacher at the college who was calling for her neighbor, Mrs. S. P. Lamb of North Pearl Street in Belton. Dr. Batte told Mitchell that Mrs. Lamb had just discharged her shotgun at a window "peeper." Only a few weeks before, someone had tried to break into the Lamb house. Mitchell was asked to come as quickly as he could, with the bloodhounds.[12]

At the time, twenty-nine-year-old Mitchell was running for re-election, and the election would take place that day. Mitchell was frequently called upon to keep the peace in Belton, because it had no police department.

Mitchell saddled his horse and rode in the dark to North Pearl Street with his bloodhounds. He talked to Mrs. Lamb, who described the shot she had taken at a black man she saw peeping into one of her windows. Mitchell's bloodhounds were unable to pick up the scent of the peeper. Mitchell returned home, expecting to investigate further at first light. But a few minutes after Mitchell got home, Dr. Batte called again to say they had found a brown derby hat and shoes near the house. Mitchell returned, but his bloodhounds for some reason refused to go near the shoes. As he and Mrs. Lamb's neighbors were talking in the moonlight, Dr. Batte noticed a black man approaching them from down the street without a hat, and she remarked, "He hasn't got on a hat, I'll bet that's the fellow." The constable quickly mounted his horse and trotted toward the man to talk to him, but he had turned the corner into 10th Avenue, and was out of sight.[13]

As Mitchell rounded the corner, he was suddenly fired upon in the dark from behind a nearby tree. The assassin fired one or two shots at the constable, one hitting him in the body. As Mrs. Lamb, Dr. Batte, and their neighbors heard the shooting and a shout, they looked up to see Mitchell's horse running toward them. The horse slowed, and Mitchell fell from its back, shouting, "Oh, Dr. Batte, Henry Gentry shot me." Dr. Batte ran to Mitchell, who repeated, "Henry Gentry shot me,"[14] then lost consciousness.

Constable Mitchell had been shot in the "back part of the side" with a shotgun, and the wound was described as large enough to "put a fist into." Dr. McElhannon was soon on the scene, saw that nothing could be done for him, and had him transported home by car. Mitchell never regained consciousness after identifying his killer, and died about 2:00 A.M. on Friday, July 22, 1910.[15]

Later that same morning, Bell County Sheriff D. C. Burkes organized a posse, including a group of police officers from Temple who had heard about the murder of Constable Mitchell and came to Belton in the early morning. Many others in the county had also heard about the murder, and by noon a crowd of two hundred to five hundred citizens had gathered to help in the search for Henry Gentry.

Henry Gentry was no stranger to lawmen in Bell County. Just two years before, he had been sentenced to two years in a Texas State Reformatory for burglary of a business in Belton. He had been released from the reformatory only a few months earlier. The Gentry family also had a reputation for causing trouble in the community. Yancy Yarborough, a former constable, told the *Temple Telegram* that he had once been called to quell a disturbance within the family, and upon arrival was jumped by all ten of them, men, women, and children. Yarborough related that he had had to knock four to the ground with his pistol before he could calm them down and make arrests.[16]

At about noon, it was reported in Belton that Henry Gentry had been seen in a nearby cornfield, and that Deputy Sheriff Dan Crow and posse members were searching the field. An unconfirmed report had also come in that a man who had been camped on the river had been killed by Gentry. The latter report proved false, but Gentry was found in the cornfield. No sooner was he spotted by the posse than he was shot and killed. His body was dragged to the edge of the field, thrown into a wagon, and driven toward Belton, where a crowd of over a thousand people had gathered. When the posse arrived in town, the crowd pulled the body out of the wagon, tossed it onto a large pile of brush, doused it with kerosene, and set it afire.[17]

In the meantime, Henry Gentry's brother and another black man had been arrested for complicity in the murder, and were in the Bell County jail. Agitators turned part of the group into a mob, who screamed for these men also to be thrown on the fire. Rushing to the jail, they were met by Sheriff Burkes and members of Constable Mitchell's family, who called for the mob to calm itself and not to harm innocent men. Walter Wilson and A. L. Curtis, brother-in-law and cousin to the dead constable respectively, asked the mob to break up, and Curtis was reported to have said that the men with him would die rather than allow the prisoners to be taken from the jail. This seemed to quiet the crowd, and they began to break up, although it would be several days before real calm returned to Belton.[18]

Constable Mitchell's family had been early settlers in Bell County, and he was not the first or the last of his family in law enforcement. His maternal grandfather was elected sheriff in Bell County in 1863, but resigned and joined the Confederate Army the following year. Constable Mitchell's widow moved to Woodward, Oklahoma, and married another peace officer, who worked for the Woodward Police Department. A son of Mitchell's daughter Agnes was chief of police in Algona, Washington, for five years, and one grandchild was married to an Oregon State Trooper. Mitchell is buried in North Belton Cemetery.[19]

Nueces County

About 2:30 A.M. on March 25, 1917, Constable Patrick W. Feely and Deputy Constable Augustin Lozano of Precinct No. 1 in Nueces County were on the hill just above the city of Corpus Christi, investigating a disturbance caused by a group of men riding around in a touring car and shouting. One of the men was riding on the hood of the car.[20]

Feely, who had served several years with the Corpus Christi police force before being elected constable, stopped the car and told the driver, Angel Gutierrez, to stop the noise. Raymond Bellamy, the man on the hood of the car, had once been a deputy sheriff, and probably recognized Feely. Lozano reported later that while Feely was talking to the driver, Bellamy hid in the bushes, and as Feely walked away, shot at him six times. Feely, shot in the stomach, fell to his knees and fired three times, wounding Bellamy in the shoulder.[21]

As was the custom of the day, Feely and Bellamy were both taken to their individual homes, and doctors attended each. Feely died about ten hours later, and on March 28, Bellamy was charged with his murder. A week later Lee Petzel replaced Feely as constable.[22]

Freestone County

Freestone County is a predominantly rural county located in East Texas on the main road between Houston and Dallas. Friday, August 9, 1918, was a typical hot day, but, as much as Charles Kilgore disliked the heat, he had other problems. Kilgore was a black man who lived near the little town of Butler in the southeast part of Freestone County. About a half-hour before, two white men had broken into his home and robbed him, and were now riding off toward Butler on a horse and a mule. Kilgore headed for the home of his constable, Bragg Dunbar, to get some help.[23]

Dunbar and Kilgore drove to Butler to intercept the robbers. Kilgore recognized the two men standing in front of Killough's Store. Dunbar told them they were under arrest for breaking into Charles Kilgore's home. As Dunbar got out of his car, Frank Wallace and his brother-in-law Alvin Henery opened fire with their rifles. Three shots hit Dunbar, killing him instantly. Kilgore took off running as Wallace and Henery also shot at him, wounding him in the hip. There were reports that a woman with them, later identified as Mrs. Frank Wallace, passed them a third rifle when they ran out of shells. When people ran out of Killough's Store to see what was going on, Wallace and Henery fired in their direction and they ran back inside.[24]

After killing Dunbar, the two men took his pistol, mounted their horse and mule, and rode off on the Rock Spring Road toward the nearby Trinity River. Just outside of Butler, they stole another horse and left the mule.[25]

Later that day, Freestone County Sheriff Jim Roper organized a posse of his deputies and about a hundred citizens and officers from nearby Leon and Anderson Counties. The next day, Saturday, they tracked Wallace and Henery across the Trinity River and into southern Anderson County. Over the next several days the posse, now including officers and citizens from Freestone and Houston Counties, trailed the two murderers. On Wednesday evening, Deputy Sheriff Parker of Anderson County was shot and slightly wounded by the fleeing men. Finally, on August 19, Wallace and Henery gave themselves up in Houston County and were returned to Freestone County by Sheriff Roper and several deputies.[26]

Two days later, a grand jury returned a true bill, and the trial began that same day in Freestone County in the 77th District Court, just twelve days after the murder of Constable Dunbar. The jury found both men guilty and sentenced them to death. The sentence was affirmed by the Texas Court of Criminal Appeals, but it was later commuted to life in prison by Governor Hobby. One of the convicted men died in prison in the 1930s, and the other escaped once, but was recaptured in West Texas and returned to prison, where he also died.[27]

It is reported that King Dunbar, a brother to slain Constable Bragg Dunbar, upon hearing about Governor Hobby's commuting of the death sentence on the two men who had killed his brother, immediately renamed his son King Bragg Dunbar. His son had formerly been named King Hobby Dunbar, after the governor.

PROHIBITION, BOOMTOWNS, AND THE DEPRESSION

From about 1910 to 1918, law-enforcement officers on Texas's southern border were mainly occupied with the spreading turmoil of the Mexican Revolution: smuggling, German-sponsored espionage, and riots. Protecting the border required the combined efforts of the Texas Rangers, local constables, and sheriff's departments, plus elements of the U.S. Army. In the other areas of the state, crime and violence were little changed.

From the end of World War I almost to the beginning of World War II, several national events greatly expanded the role of law enforcement throughout the nation and Texas, but also acted to corrupt many police agencies. The first of these incidents was Prohibition, which began with the ratification of the Volstead Act in 1919, and ended fourteen years later with its repeal in 1933. It left in its wake an entrenched group of crime families, some of which are active to this day.

Another major event, which shaped Texas more than most other places, was the discovery of large amounts of crude oil there in the 1920s and 1930s. This gave birth to a whole new industry and created abundant jobs for many educated and uneducated men and women; but it also created boomtowns, which sprang up around the drilling rigs and quickly became centers of violence, crime, and corruption. The new market for crude oil was, of course, the result of the sudden proliferation of automobiles after the invention of the internal combustion engine.[28]

Perhaps the most traumatic and life-changing event of the period was the stock market crash in 1929, followed by the Great Depression of the 1930s, which helped spawn a series of "mad-dog" criminals, violent labor strikes, and a more transient and rootless population. Armed robbery and murder became the crimes of the day.[29]

Dallas County

Garland is one of the small Texas towns that have now been absorbed into the large Dallas–Fort Worth metropolitan area. In 1924, however, Garland was still a small town relying on county law enforcement, such as constables and deputy sheriffs, to keep the peace. E. J. "Lige" Harris was a longtime, highly respected constable in the Dallas County Precinct, which included the town of Garland.

On Tuesday night, September 2, 1924, Harris was making his usual rounds on the square in the center of Garland. He had just turned the corner near Dyer Drugstore when he was shot in the stomach several times by a person or persons unknown. The area was deserted, and Harris knew he was seriously wounded. He broke the window of the *Garland Morning News* to use the telephone and summon help. (It was a coincidence that his sister was the telephone operator who answered his call for help.) Harris died some forty hours later, on September 4, 1924.[30]

Within hours, several people were arrested or held as material witnesses in the shooting. The newspapers reported that Dallas County sheriff's deputies suspected that Constable Harris was shot by one or more black men, and six people, all black, were arrested. An automatic pistol suspected by sheriff's deputies to be the gun that shot Harris was allegedly found near White Rock Lake but was never tied to the shooting. No one was charged with the shooting, and all were released from custody.[31]

Fred Harris, son of Constable Lige Harris, reported that his family did not believe the story circulated by the Dallas County law

Wooden derricks and close spacing in an early Texas oil field (courtesy East Texas Photo Collection, the Center for American History, Austin).

enforcement community involving the black suspects. The Ku Klux Klan was very active in that area at the time, and his father was an outspoken opponent of the group. The family thought it was more likely that Klan members were responsible for the murder of Constable Harris, and the arrest of innocent blacks was to deflect suspicion from the Klan.[32]

Taylor County

In March 1925, Howard County Sheriff W. W. Satterwhite arrived in Taylor County searching for Lopez Morales, a Mexican national wanted for questioning about several crimes, including a murder in Howard County. Satterwhite had information that Morales was hiding out near Merkel, a town in northwest Young County, and asked George L. Reeves, who was constable from the Merkel area and a deputy sheriff in Young County, to assist him in searching for the man.[33]

About 11:00 in the morning of March 24, Reeves and Satterwhite found Morales in a squatters camp near Merkel. Morales, who had several guns, including a rifle, fired on them. The two lawmen carried only pistols. Reeves was seriously wounded. Satterwhite was cut off from his police car by the gunfire, and he ran to a nearby farm to borrow a car so he could go summon help. Satterwhite was running to that car when Morales shot him. As Satterwhite lay on the ground wounded, Morales shot him again, killing him, then walked back to where Reeves lay wounded and shot him in the head, killing him also.[34]

When the murders became known later that day, some two hundred Merkel-area citizens formed a posse to hunt Morales and another man who had joined him at the camp. By the next day, the posse had grown to about five hundred law-enforcement officers and citizens. Morales and his companion were seen in the area back toward Abilene, and the search moved in that direction.

Late on March 26, Abilene Chief of Police Robert Burch, Deputy Chief Lige Jennings, and several of the posse searched a rail siding near Abilene. There, Morales, hiding in a boxcar, shot and wounded Jennings. The posse threw dynamite under the boxcar, blowing it apart and wounding Morales and his companion. Both were then shot and killed by the crowd and taken back to Abilene, tied on the fender of the police chief's car.[35]

Tarrant County

Just before Christmas in 1925, Tarrant County Constable Robert F. Poe and Deputy Constable Edward Finch went to the home of Manuel L. Carson in Fort Worth to investigate the theft of automobile tires. Carson had recently been released from jail, where he had served a sixty-day federal sentence for possession and sale of intoxicating liquor.[36]

Constable Poe and Carson spoke in front of Carson's house at about 6:30 P.M. on Wednesday, December 23, 1925. Deputy Finch moved toward the house to search for the missing tires. He had just reached the top of the porch steps when he heard a shot, and saw that Carson had shot Constable Poe. As Poe dropped to the ground dead, Finch ran to Carson and pulled the gun from his hands. Carson ran away, and Finch fired three shots at him, killing him instantly. At the inquest the next day, Finch was cleared of any wrongdoing in Carson's death.[37]

Young County

At about 4:00 P.M on November 18, 1929, Mrs. John Reese walked into the Olney Police Department asking for protection from her husband, John, who she said had threatened her life. Forty-four-year-old Young County Constable Edward Lankford met with Mrs. Reese to take her complaint. As Lankford was taking the information, John Reese entered the police office. Lankford asked him to retract the threat on his wife, and asked Reese if he was armed. Reese pulled a .38-caliber pistol from his pocket and shot Lankford, striking him in the heart, then ran out of the police office, but surrendered a few minutes later to Police Chief Anderson. Reese was transported to the jail at Graham, the county seat of Young County. He was later convicted of the murder of Constable Lankford.[38]

Henderson County

Jess Sweeten served as constable in Henderson County from 1929 to 1931, during the Depression and the East Texas oil boom. It was his first law-enforcement job. As he describes it, the job primarily required that he be "man enough to keep the drunks out of the street, the bullies. You had about 2,500 to 3,000 iron workers, steam fitters, and boilermakers that were concentrated down there, and there was no roads in but dirt roads, in and out. They couldn't get out of there in wet weather. And it was rough—drunks on the street, fighting."[39]

Sweeten has been called a colorful and controversial lawman, probably because he shot nine men as a peace officer, killing three of them. Once he was called to a rural area, where a man had barricaded himself in his house, shooting at people and cars as they drove past. When he arrived at the house, Sweeten walked up on the porch out of sight of the shooter and listened for the man to move around. Sweeten knew that he could tell where the shooter was in the old creaky house. When the man moved, he kicked the door open and shot the armed man three times with his .45 automatic.[40]

Constable Sweeten went on to serve as sheriff of Henderson County from 1933 to 1955. During that time Sweeten solved several high-profile crimes, including twenty-one murder cases and at least one kidnapping. After that, from 1955 to 1970, he worked as a special investigator for Mobil Oil Company. At one point, he was also elected mayor of Athens, Texas.[41]

Williamson County

Fifty-one-year-old Sam M. Moore had served the people of Williamson County for two terms as county commissioner when he was elected constable in 1932. Moore was not experienced in law enforcement. His precinct contained mostly rural Williamson County east of the main highway from Austin to Waco. Granger was the largest town in the precinct.

On November 14, 1933, thirty-eight-year-old Lewis Cernoch was tried by jury and found guilty in Justice John Nunn's court on a misdemeanor charge of causing a disturbance and using abusive language to a woman. He was fined $28.05. Cernoch said he did not have the money, and the court gave him ten days to pay his fine. Within a few days, however, he left town.

He returned three months later, in early February 1934.[42] When Constable Moore heard Cernoch was back in Williamson County, he approached him with an arrest warrant, but Cernoch ran and didn't stop until Moore pulled his gun. Cernoch then said he would accompany Moore, if he could bring his employer. Moore agreed to this request, and allowed Cernoch to go to his room to change into cleaner clothes and pick up his coat, as it was a very cold day. It was probably at that time that Cernoch armed himself with a Luger pistol he had brought home from Germany after the war. Moore knew nothing about the gun. He returned to Granger in his car, picking up City Marshal Lindsey (who had previously worked as a deputy sheriff and a constable) on the way. Cernoch followed in a second car with his employer. All went to Justice Nunn's court.

In court, Cernoch again claimed he did not have the money to pay the $28.05 fine and court costs. He was sentenced to some time in the county jail. Lindsey led the way out of the court, with Cernoch behind, followed by Moore.[43]

As they walked out of the court, Cernoch shoved Lindsey, then shot him once. Then he shot Moore, hitting him in the left hand, his gun hand. Moore picked up his pistol with his other hand and fired once at Cernoch. The shot missed. Before he could fire again, Cernoch shot him four times in the body, head, and arm. Moore dropped on the lawn mortally wounded.[44]

But Cernoch was not through. He went back to Lindsey and shot him several more times. He then returned to Justice Nunn's court, and fired several times at Nunn and Assistant Criminal District Attorney M. B. Colbert, wounding Nunn in the leg. Cernoch finally ran out of bullets and began to reload his gun. During this time, Colbert talked to him for several minutes. Then Cernoch turned and abruptly left the office. He walked a short way down the street, stopped, calmly lit his pipe, and continued to reload his pistol.[45]

Within a few minutes, some brave citizens of Granger distracted Cernoch, knocked him to the ground and disarmed him. At his arraignment the next day, it is said that Cernoch remembered the minute details of the murders the day before, and said that he had committed the deed "because he had been double-crossed, and he was not going to jail (just) because he had no money."[46]

As customary at that time, Cernoch's trial for the murder of City Marshal Lindsey took place less than a month later. Testimony took just two days; the jury deliberated about twelve hours; and Cernoch was sentenced to die in the electric chair. He was not tried for the murder of Constable Moore and the two assault charges because of the sentencing in the first trial. Less than a month later, Cernoch's appeal for a new trial was denied.[47]

If the two peace officers made a mistake, it was in allowing Cernoch to go alone into his room, where he apparently armed himself with a deadly weapon. Apparently neither Constable Moore nor Marshal Lindsey searched Cernoch for a weapon after he arrived at the hearing, but who would expect a man to kill two peace officers, and attempt to kill two court officials, over a $28.05 fine? Lewis Cernoch did, and as a result, he died in the electric chair.

Wharton County

T. W. "Buckshot" Lane was elected constable in Precinct No. 1 in Wharton County in 1931. He served as constable for eight years, and in 1941 was elected sheriff of the county, and held that office for twelve years. Interviewed by Thad Sitton in 1986, Lane remembered that in the 1930s, "The constable had as much authority as a sheriff, only he had a small precinct. . . . They had the same authority as the sheriff, but mainly they served papers . . . . Some constables took it on themselves to enforce the law. I enforced the law in my precinct."[48]

Lane went on to explain: "The county was wide open when I came to office. There was slot machines and there was whorehouses. . . . When I got in, I told 'em that these places had to stop. . . . We had four clean counties in there. Besides Wharton, Jackson County was clean, Matagorda was clean, and Calhoun was clean. The Highway Patrol would help me, too."

"During the bootleg days, I had bought a lot of whiskey, drank a lot of whiskey. But I told these fellows, I said, 'Now fellows, when I'm elected an officer, you gonna have to go out of business.' . . . The sheriff over in Fort Bend County was selling it out of the jailhouse. But my people quit—they knew I meant business with 'em."[49]

Buckshot Lane also told the story about how he came to burn down an abandoned highway bridge in 1934. Kentleton Bridge in Wharton County was not removed when the state built Highway 59 with a new bridge. Thirteen people were killed because they missed the turn onto the new bridge, and when the state of Texas failed to correct the problem, Constable Lane decided to do something about it. He simply burned the old bridge down. The next day, he went to Austin. There he met Homer Garrison, then head of the Department of Public Safety and the Texas Rangers. Garrison said to him, "What the hell are you doing here? I just sent two Rangers to Wharton County to find out who burned that bridge last night. You ought to be there helping." Constable Lane, of course, returned immediately to help the Rangers investigate the bridge burning. District Attorney Bob Bassett announced that he would buy the finest suit of clothes that money could buy for the man who burned the bridge, but he would still have to prosecute him. Ten years later, after the statute of limitations ran out for arson, Lane told Bassett that he owed him a new set of clothes. Bassett's immediate response: "You SOB. I knew you were the one who burnt the bridge."[50]

Montgomery County

Clint Peoples had been a deputy sheriff in Montgomery County for almost two years when, in February 1933, he resigned to become chief deputy constable of Precinct No. 7, where George Washington "Uncle George" Templeton, the long-time constable, had asked Peoples to assist him.[51] Templeton had been constable for almost thirty years in Montgomery County, but things were changing, as recent oil discoveries near Conroe had brought many lawbreakers into the county.

Later in 1933, Chief Deputy Peoples also accepted an appointment as a Special Texas Ranger. To many this was the equivalent of receiving a Little Orphan Annie Secret Decoder Badge, but it helped Peoples supplement his uncertain income from fees as a constable, by allowing him also to work as an investigator for several oil companies and the Texas Racing Commission. He later resigned this appointment.

Special Texas Rangers were the result of the election of an incompetent, corrupt state government in Texas, which came into being when Miriam "Ma" Ferguson was elected governor. After her election, Ferguson was upset because most of the Texas Rangers had publicly supported her opponent. She fired all of the current Texas Rangers and reorganized the group with people who had little or no law enforcement experience and renamed them Special Texas Rangers. Furthermore, Ferguson sold many of the five thousand Special Texas Rangers appointments. As a result, there were many abuses of police powers by those appointees.[52]

Peoples described his job as chief deputy constable this way: "[Templeton] kept me awfully, awfully busy, so my routine changed from a considerably slow one to a fast pace." He was right, for the Precinct 7 constable's office in the 1930s was just about as busy as the county sheriff's office, because most of the criminal activity was

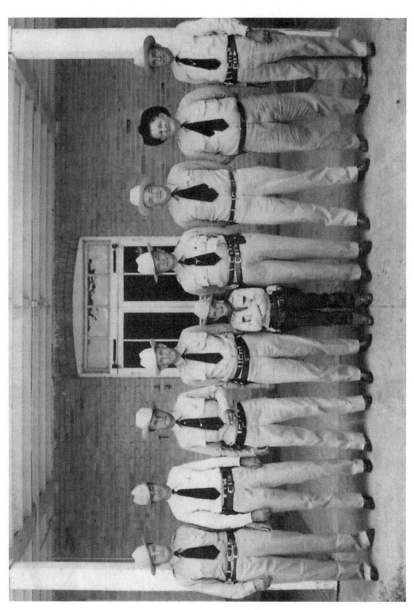

Clint Peoples, shown here on far left, served as chief deputy constable in Montgomery County, Texas. Photo of Texas Rangers Headquarters Company at Camp Mabry, Austin, 1951 (courtesy Texas Ranger Museum, Waco, Texas).

in Precinct 7. Among the many stories told about Templeton and his chief deputy is one about the time both drove out to a home where they knew home brew was being made, but had never been able to prove it. After almost a half-hour searching the premises and finding nothing, Peoples heard a loud pop, and the ceiling began to leak a familiar-smelling liquid. Templeton (whose eyesight was poor) climbed the "disappearing staircase" into the poorly lit attic and called to Peoples, "Come here and look, son, these things are completely full of horse turds." It turned out that the brewmaster had used dried peaches for color and flavor in the home brew, and these peaches were what "Uncle George" had seen in the attic.[53]

Only once did Clint Peoples use his gun while he was chief deputy constable. One night he and a deputy were looking for some thieves around Conroe. As they walked down the street they spotted a Model A Roadster, a car said to belong to the thieves. Just then, it suddenly lurched backward and a loud bang was heard. Peoples was sure it was a shotgun he heard and fired a shot at the car as it sped away. Later that night, the hospital called and said they were treating a man for a gunshot wound. Peoples went to talk to the man, who confessed that he and the car's driver were responsible for several thefts. The shot Peoples fired toward the disappearing Model A had blown away his jaw. Both the wounded man and the driver went to jail.[54]

After Peoples spent almost five years as chief deputy constable in Montgomery County, Constable Templeton said that he would re-sign his office if Peoples would accept the job. However, Peoples had something else in mind. He had already had a chance to observe and work with several of the new Texas Rangers, who had come to Montgomery County to work near the oil boomtown. As a result, he had decided he wanted to work for the real Texas Rangers, who by now were a part of the Department of Public Safety. To join the Texas Rangers at that time, candidates had to have experience both as a peace officer and in the Department of Public Safety. Peoples re-signed as chief deputy constable in 1937 and joined the Sheriff's De-partment for four years, until November 1941. He then joined the Highway Patrol, a part of the Department of Public Safety, prior to joining the Texas Rangers.[55]

Peoples was a very well known and respected Texas Ranger until his retirement. Like many other respected lawmen, he began his law-enforcement career as a deputy constable.

143

Big changes were occurring in Texas in the late 1930s, with the repeal of Prohibition and, in some areas, a lessening of the effects of the Great Depression. But jobs were still hard to find, and many a young man at the time enlisted in the armed forces, for another World War had started in Europe. In 1941, when the United States entered that war, law enforcement took a back seat to the war effort, and until the war was over in 1946, police forces made up of older officers were normal in most jurisdictions.

Chapter VIII
Modern Texas,
1946 to 1999

More Constables at Risk

With the end of World War II and the settling-in of the Cold War, law enforcement returned to coping with everyday crime and violence. But during the last half of the twentieth century, crime and law enforcement have changed as dramatically as society, and morals. In Texas, assaults on and murders of constables had risen alarmingly by the end of the 1970s. Despite dramatic advances in communications, however, the exploits of many individual constables do not receive a lot of publicity. By looking closely at those constables killed in the line of duty from the late 1940s to the end of the century, it is possible to grasp the range of activities, responsibilities, and risks typical of the office, as well as the dedication and service of many Texas constables.

Duval County

About 10:30 P.M. on August 4, 1961, Duval County Sheriff Vidal Garcia was notified that someone was seen burglarizing the home of Oscar Garcia about two blocks southeast of the Duval County Court House, in San Diego. The sheriff radioed for backup and proceeded to the home of Oscar Garcia, who was known to be away, vacationing in Washington state. When Sheriff Garcia arrived, he heard noises inside the home and called out for the person inside to come out of the house. An eighteen-year-old youth known to the sheriff, Guadalupe Guajardo, crawled out of a broken window and told the sheriff he was in the home "looking for ammunition."[1]

About that time Constable Pedro R. Sendejo, San Diego Police Chief Daniel De La Rosa, and Deputy Sheriff Manuel Amayo arrived at the scene to assist the sheriff. Sheriff Garcia turned Guajardo over to Sendejo and De La Garza, while he and Deputy Amayo went into the house to make sure no one else was inside. Constable Sendejo took charge of the burglar, and as he walked him toward his vehicle, he asked Guajardo to take his hands out of his pockets. As Guajardo withdrew his hands from his pockets, he pulled a .22-caliber revolver on the constable and fired two bullets into Sendejo's chest. Sendejo took two steps and fell dead. Guajardo quickly ran to his home in the next block, then surrendered to the officers who followed him. Pedro Sendejo was forty-one years old. Before being elected constable of Precinct No. 1 just nine months earlier, he had been a deputy sheriff for two years. Sendejo was a veteran of World War II, a rancher, and father to one daughter and four sons.[2]

At the bond hearing later that month, it was determined that Guajardo actually shot Constable Sendejo in the heart with only one bullet, as the second one was a .22-caliber ratshot that caused only a surface wound. The shooting had actually occurred in the part of San Diego that lay in Jim Wells County. As a result Guajardo was indicted by the Jim Wells County Grand Jury for capital murder.[3]

Ellis County

In 1948, Sergeant Ben Wicker retired from the Dallas Police Department, married the secretary of the police chief, and moved to Ellis County, just south of Dallas. It wasn't too long before Ben Wicker ran for constable, was elected, and spent the next fourteen years in that position. On September 22, 1962, Constable Wicker went to a barbershop in the small town of Ferris in his precinct to arrest thirty-year-old Bobby Bradford for discharging a pistol inside the town limits.[4]

As constables and other peace officers have arrested many in trail towns for the same offense for almost one hundred years, Wicker may not have been overly apprehensive about discharging his duty in this case. Yet as Constable Wicker tried to make his arrest in the barbershop, Bradford pulled a gun and started shooting. Wicker and Bradford each fired six shots at close range, hitting not only each other but also a bystander. After the shooting, Constable Wicker, even though shot several times, appeared to be recovering favorably, but died twenty days later from complications from his wounds in a Waxahachie hospital. Bradford recovered and was charged with murder. Constable Ben Wicker was a highly regarded peace officer in north Texas. At his funeral, a sheriff, two police chiefs, and four other officers from Dallas and Ellis Counties served as pallbearers.[5]

Atascosa County

Approximately 10:00 P.M., June 13, 1965, fifty-five-year-old Constable George Hindes waved to Sheriff H. H. Howard of Atascosa County as he left a dance in Charlotte to patrol his precinct. He had not driven very far south on Highway 97, when an erratically driven green pickup caught his attention. Thinking the driver might be drunk, Hindes turned off to follow the pickup a short block to where it stopped at the Sanchez Tavern on the edge of town.

Constable Hindes approached the driver, Elias Garcia. Witnesses stated that the constable suggested to Garcia that he go home, because he had obviously already had too much to drink. Garcia initially argued, but then agreed to leave. He asked Constable Hindes to find his wife and ask her to come to the car. Hindes complied, and as he and Margarita Garcia came out of the bar, Elias stepped out of the pickup and shot the constable seven times with a .22-caliber rifle. Hindes never had the chance to draw his own pistol. He died immediately.[6]

The murderer and his wife drove quickly away. Sheriff Howard and a deputy arrived a few minutes later and called to stop a 1950 green Ford pickup. Roadblocks were quickly set up. Elias Garcia was an itinerant farm worker who had been employed for about a month on a nearby farm, but by the time Deputy Murray Potts and Trooper Gene Powell of the Highway Patrol reached his home, Garcia had already left.[7]

Some fifty-five miles south, LaSalle County Sheriff Frank Newman, Deputy Jack Curtis, DPS Trooper Harlan Schroeder, and Texas Ranger Jack Van Cleve had set up a road block at the junction of Highways 81 and 97 outside of Cotulla. Before long, they saw the pickup pull into a Humble gas station. Garcia got out, purchased a road map, and asked for directions to the town of Roma, on the Mexican border. The officers converged on Garcia. When Sheriff Newman spoke to him, Garcia broke and ran behind a welding shop, across the railroad tracks, and into a field, where he attempted to hide. Garcia and his wife were both apprehended, and the rifle he had shot Constable Hindes with was found on the floorboard of the pickup.[8]

Constable Hindes had lived all his life in Atascosa County, as had his father and grandfather, who had been killed by Indians just two months short of a hundred years before George Hindes was killed. His family had first settled in the county in the 1850s. George Hindes had served several years as Atascosa County's chief deputy sheriff, but had been elected constable only eighteen months.[9]

No one was surprised when Elias Garcia was indicted a few weeks later on a charge of murder with malice by the Atascosa Grand Jury. Everyone was surprised, however, when his fingerprints proved his true identity was Sixto DeLeon, fugitive from another murder charge in Bailey County in the Texas Panhandle. DeLeon had killed his own brother-in-law, Juan Robles, by shooting him in the temple with a .22-caliber pistol exactly one year before he murdered Constable Hindes. He had escaped from the jail in Muleshoe, Texas, on September 1, 1964, and had been on the run ever since. In addition, DeLeon was wanted as a parole violator in Wisconsin, where the thirty-four-year-old had served two prison terms.[10]

On July 6, 1965, less than one month after he had murdered Constable Hindes, Sixto DeLeon was sentenced to ninety-nine years in the Texas prison system. The entire court proceedings took less than four hours, and the jury deliberated less than ten minutes.[11]

A TIME OF KILLING

The 1970s was a rough decade for Texas constables. Eight constables and deputy constables—almost thirty-three percent of those killed in the line of duty in Texas in the last hundred years—were murdered. This far exceeds the number killed in any other state during that period.[12]

Orange County

Lewis O. Ford was elected constable of Precinct No. 3 in Orange County in 1968. Before that, he was deputy constable, and earlier an Orange County deputy sheriff for fifteen years. He also held a full-time position in the Firestone Tire and Rubber plant in Orange, Texas. On January 31, 1971, a Sunday night, Constable Ford was in his car when he heard Deputy Sheriff Ronnie Reeves report that he was giving chase to a suspected intoxicated driver who refused to stop. Lewis Ford joined the chase, and as the car slowed, Ford pulled in front to block its path.[13]

The driver of the car, twenty-six-year-old George W. Burch, was drunk and belligerent. He refused to cooperate with the officers and began to fight when they attempted to detain him. When Deputy Reeves grabbed Burch, Constable Ford moved to assist. Burch caught Ford in the neck with a karate-like hand chop, and Ford collapsed. Two DPS troopers arrived and took Burch into custody, while Deputy Reeves attempted to revive the fallen constable. Ford was transported to Doctor's Hospital in nearby Groves, but never regained consciousness. The forty-four-year-old constable, who had been chosen by the Bridge City Optimist Club as Law-Enforcement Officer of the Year for 1970, died as the result of the assault by George W. Burch.[14]

The Orange County Grand Jury determined that Ford had suffered a heart attack as the result of the blow to his neck. Because Ford had had a heart attack about four months earlier, they did not indict Burch for murder. They did indict him for negligent homicide, driving while intoxicated, and unlawfully carrying a firearm, but the charges were later dropped. Constable Lewis O. Ford was replaced as constable in Precinct No. 3 by his brother John A. Ford,[15] who was first appointed, and then subsequently elected and reelected to the job for more than seventeen years. He was still serving as constable in Precinct No. 3 in 1999.

Hill County

Like a number of constables, Milton C. Boortz held two jobs in law enforcement at the same time. He was city marshal of tiny Malone and a constable in Hill County. In addition, he was also a Dallas fireman. On Thursday evening, March 25, 1971, Constable Boortz, and DPS Trooper Fred Beall were in the constable's vehicle making rounds, when a car with its license plate obscured was seen speeding out of Malone. The two lawmen gave chase for about five miles before the car stopped. The driver was called back to the constable's car. In a few minutes, the driver and Constable Boortz walked forward together toward the vehicle to talk with its two passengers. Trooper Beall was walking toward the stopped car on the opposite side when he saw Constable Boortz begin to draw his

Constable Lewis O. Ford, Orange County, died in the line of duty on January 31, 1971 (photo courtesy of Constable Ford's family).

pistol. Within seconds a shot from the car felled Boortz. The driver jumped into the car and sped off. Trooper Beall fired eight rounds from his pistol at the fleeing car and blew out the back windshield.[16]

Constable Milton Boortz had been fatally shot in the head. Trooper Beall sounded the alarm and peace officers from all over north central Texas began looking for the vehicle and the three suspects. They discovered that the three men in the vehicle had robbed a liquor store in Malone just prior to the shooting. Constable Boortz and Trooper Beall had been unaware of the robbery when they began the car chase. Benny Walker was arrested in Dallas for the murder of Constable Milton Boortz.[17]

Camp County

Waple Parker lived in the small town of Pittsburg, in northeast Texas, and had spent more than ten of his sixty-one years in mental hospitals. His brother said, "He was afraid of people. There were times when he'd be all right and then he'd get to talking about foolish crazy things. Things that never happened. It was his imagination. He was really afraid of officers. . . . He carried a gun with him wherever he went. I don't think he'd leave without it."

It was obvious that Parker's family were afraid of him, and they had good reason to be. They had filed a request for commitment order asking for a medical and mental examination of Waple only a few weeks before.[18]

But Camp County Constable Dan Tubbs was in the hospital himself the week the request was issued. His deputy Noble Smith and County Attorney L. E. Bell had both been out to the house and saw no way to get between Waple Parker and his guns. That commitment order would just have to wait until a better opportunity presented itself. To Constable Tubbs that meant when serving it would not endanger anyone involved. On Thursday, June 29, 1972, however, Tubbs received a call about a disturbance at the Parker home on Dukes Chapel Road in northeast Pittsburg. He drove to the house, but did not go inside. Because no shots had been fired and no real problem was apparent, he soon left the area. That night, however, a call came in reporting that someone was shooting at houses on Dukes Chapel Road.[19]

Tubbs was the first officer on the scene, and must have been very apprehensive as he pulled up in front of the Parker home and saw

Waple Parker, who was in the street, wave his gun, then run into his house. Tubbs never got out of the vehicle, nor did he have a chance to call for help on his radio. Before Tubbs could act, Waple Parker fired his rifle from the window of his home, killing Tubbs where he sat. Parker also shot at police officer Hardy Griffin, second on the scene, hitting his patrol car once. Soon several officers were at the Parker home on Dukes Chapel Road. As they tried to talk Waple Parker out of his home, he slipped out of the back door and disappeared.[20]

The death of Constable Dan Tubbs was tragic, but what followed a few hours later was even more tragic. On Friday morning, a Texas Ranger, searching for the escaped killer of Constable Tubbs, shot and killed a mentally retarded man whose description was similar to Parker's. The ranger found the man hiding behind a rural mailbox and carrying a pistol. When the man refused to put his gun down, the Ranger fired an unheeded warning shot, then killed the man with one shot. The man turned out to be Walker Curtis, who was known to be mentally retarded, and was carrying a toy gun.[21]

A few hours later, Waple Parker was captured without incident. Owing to his history of mental illness, and previous confinement in a mental hospital, Parker was committed to a Texas State Hospital for the Criminally Insane.[22]

Pecos County

Pecos County is as arid as any area in West Texas, and no place to take a walk. So when two men with forty-three pounds of marijuana in their vehicle led officers on a twelve-mile high-speed chase that ended with the capture of one of the two on a dead-end street in Ozona, law enforcement in Pecos County expected the other fugitive would try to escape by another vehicle. They quickly set up a roadblock on U.S. Highway 290, west of Ozona. Allen Graham, constable of Precinct No. 6 in Pecos County, had been a longtime deputy sheriff in Pecos County. As was natural, he and a number of other law-enforcement officers participated in manning the roadblock. About 6:00 A.M. on the morning of September 18, 1973, Constable Graham was helping check a truck stopped at the roadblock, when he was struck by a car coming toward the roadblock from the other direction. The driver of that vehicle had for some reason not slowed sufficiently to see Allen Graham in the roadway, although he claimed that he was blinded by the truck's headlights. Graham was taken to the hospital, but was dead on arrival.[23]

Tarrant County

Earl "Andy" Andrews had been in law enforcement for more than twenty-three years. During that time, his wife Borta said, "Andy never turned off the (police) radio." Andy had served with the Fort Worth Police Department, as chief of police in Mansfield, and a deputy constable, before he was elected constable in Tarrant County's Precinct No. 8.[24]

That was only about a year and a half before Constable Andrews and his wife, herself a reserve deputy constable, traveled to South Texas on a vacation in June 1975. On June 7, they had left Victoria and were proceeding back home to Mansfield. As they drove toward Hallettsville on Highway 77, the police radio in the Andrews car broadcast a request to all law enforcement officers around Victoria to be on the lookout for a van that had been involved in a hit-and-run accident. The dispatcher then broadcast the license number. To Andy's amazement the vehicle just in front of him fit the van's description and the license numbers were a match. Constable Andrews called the dispatcher and said, "I got the van you are looking for." When the dispatcher asked, "Can you stop it?" Andy proceeded to do just that. As he walked toward the van, he saw two young men in the front seat, and called for them to get out of the vehicle. The driver hesitated, but the passenger opened his door and got out. Andy's wife was sitting in the front seat of their car, and saw the passenger slide the van's side door open. The passenger reached into the van and came out with a 20-gauge shotgun. Constable Andrews must have also seen these movements on the other side of the van, because by now he had his gun out of his holster, and shouted, "Drop that gun!"[25]

As the passenger stepped from behind the van, he shot Constable Andrews in the abdomen. As Andrews dropped to the highway, the gunman kept pointing the shotgun as he walked toward him. Borta Andrews knew what was about to happen and screamed, "Don't shoot him again!" "Don't shoot him again!" But the killer shoved the shotgun against Andy's prostrate body and shot him in the chest. As Borta Andrews screamed once more, "Don't shoot him again," the killer swung around, leveled the shotgun at the car, and

Constable Earl F. Andrews, Tarrant County, killed in the line of duty in Lavaca County on June 7, 1975 (photo courtesy of Mrs. Earl Andrews).

fired the weapon at her. Instinctively, she ducked to her left. As the windshield blew out in her face, she was hit in the right shoulder, and a few pellets hit her face. The perpetrators thought they had killed both of the Andrewses, and sped away.[26]

Both killers were captured quickly, and found guilty. In the trial, it was revealed that both men had outstanding arrest warrants. The gunman was sentenced to ninety-nine years in Texas prisons.

Constable Andrews was just forty-nine years old when he was murdered on the highway north of Victoria for stopping a car on what he had been told was a hit-and-run offense.[27]

Zapata County

Manuel Gonzalez was elected constable in Zapata County's Precinct No. 1 in 1972. Before that he had been a sheriff's deputy for almost ten years. By the mid-1970s, Zapata County was not a place to get into trouble with the Sheriff's Department. Zapata County deputies were known for their lack of humor and strict compliance with the law. Oligario Villareal had had several run-ins with sheriff's deputies, and carried a grudge against anyone with a badge.[28]

In 1976, Constable Gonzalez, now forty-three years old, and Deputy Jorge Gutierrez went into business together and opened a pool hall and lounge in Zapata County. About 8:00 P.M. on January 20, 1977, Constable Gonzalez stopped by the lounge to take a break and play a quick game of pool. A few minutes later Oligario Villareal, who was on probation, walked in. As Constable Gonzalez leaned over the pool table, Villareal drew a .22-caliber pistol from his pocket and shot Gonzalez in the head. Manuel Gonzalez fell to the floor, dead, and Villareal ran from the lounge.[29]

Three days later, Oligario Villareal was captured in nearby Webb County, and returned to Zapata County, where he was tried and convicted for Gonzalez's murder. Villareal was sentenced to twenty years in Texas penitentiaries, but served only thirteen years before he was released. He returned to Zapata County. Only a few months after his return, Villareal was stopped for a traffic violation by the Highway Patrol and in an ensuing confrontation, was shot and killed by a DPS Trooper.[30]

Constable Manuel Gonzalez was survived by a large family. His daughters and sons all graduated from college and are still living along the Rio Grande. Gonzalez's wife still resides in Zapata, and his

mother lives in the town of New Lupeno. The constable is still remembered in Zapata County.

Dallas County

Joe Mack Cox had been in law enforcement for most of his adult
life. Cox was a retired Liquor Control Board agent before he joined
Dallas County Precinct No. 1 as a deputy constable. On Friday afternoon, September 22, 1978, another deputy constable, Gary Edwards, contacted Cox to request his assistance early Monday morning in serving a writ of attachment on defendant Larry Rocher, who
had failed to respond to a prior civil court summons.[31]

Early on the morning of September 25, 1978, Deputy Constables
Edwards and Cox went to Rocher's residence to serve the writ, but
Rocher refused to come out or let the deputies into his home, so no
levy could take place on Rocher's property. They then asked Rocher
to come to the constable's office later in the day, but his attitude
betrayed his lack of sincerity in showing up in their office. For that
reason, Cox and Edwards each positioned their vehicles to watch
Rocher's residence to see when he left his home.[32]

After a short time Rocher did leave the house, get into his vehicle,
and drive away. Deputy Constables Cox and Edwards signaled for
him to stop, but he refused. A five-mile, high-speed pursuit ensued.
Apparently deciding he was not going to get away from the two
officers, Rocher pulled into a parking lot at the intersection of Coit
Road and Beltline in North Dallas. Both constables were agitated,
and Edwards later remarked that Cox looked shaky. Cox soon appeared to calm down, however. He told Rocher to get into the patrol car and that he would drive him to Precinct No. 1 headquarters
to serve the writ of attachment.

By this time Rocher was cooperative, and sat in the front seat with
Joe Cox, while Deputy Edwards prepared to follow. The vehicle
driven by Cox had moved just a few feet, when Edwards noticed
Cox's head drop back on the seat. Rocher looked toward Joe Cox,
and then back at Edwards several times. Cox had suffered a massive
heart attack and died. It was his second attack in six months. Edwards and Rocher attempted to revive Cox, with Edwards performing CPR until the ambulance arrived.[33]

Hidalgo County

Former Justice of the Peace Reynaldo Ruiz lived near the junction of Los Ebanos Road and Washington Avenue, just inside the city limits of Mission, in Hidalgo County. Early on the morning of February 17, 1979, he awakened to several people's arguing on the road outside and a single gun shot. Judge Ruiz went outside and found a patrol car with its lights and engine still running. The body of Reserve Deputy Constable Ricky Steven Lewis was lying next to the vehicle. Twenty-three-year-old Lewis had been shot once in the chest and was dead.[34]

Deputy Constable Lewis was found lying on a .357 Magnum pistol. His own weapon, a .41 Magnum revolver, was missing. It appeared that after a traffic stop, someone argued with the officer, then shot and killed him, stealing his weapon before fleeing the area. One can only guess how the other weapon got under Lewis's body, but it is possible that he was shot by one person after disarming another. When Lewis fell, the two perpetrators may have panicked, and unable to find their own gun, snatched Lewis's from his holster as Judge Ruiz turned on his house lights. The family, friends, and citizens of Hidalgo County established a reward fund for the arrest and conviction of a person or persons responsible for the murder. The reward was never collected, and the killer or killers of Deputy Constable Ricky Lewis are still at large in 1999.[35]

Nueces County

Patrick S. Runyon was deputy constable of Precinct No. 6, a mostly rural area of western Nueces County. There had been some heavy rains in part of his precinct, and on the night of February 7, 1981, he received a complaint that a red pickup was driving across a number of lawns, trenching them, and causing property damage. Deputy Constable Runyon, along with Deputy Sheriffs Samuel T. Gomez and Michael Allen responded to the call. They drove to the community of Annaville, just outside of the city limits of Corpus Christi. Runyon believed the described vehicle belonged to the occupants of a house at 2515 Sundown Lane. He knocked on the door several times before it was opened only slightly. Deputy Gomez testified that Runyon identified himself and told nineteen-year-old

Stephen Calaway, who had answered the door, that he was investigating a destruction of property complaint.[36]

Gomez said he heard the person behind the door curse Runyon, telling him to "get off my property," and threatening to use a .357 Magnum. When Runyon responded that he "didn't come to cause violence," more cursing and another demand to get off the property followed. Deputy Gomez testified Runyon was then pulled into the house, and shot with a .22-caliber handgun. Deputies Gomez and Allen rushed up on the porch, where Stephen Calaway shot at Gomez from the kitchen door.[37]

Stephen Calaway, nineteen years old, and his brother Douglas Calaway, twenty-one years old, were both later arrested at home, after being subdued by Precinct No. 6 Constable Bill Bode and other law enforcement officers. They were charged with capital murder in the death of Deputy Constable Runyon. Stephen Calaway was also charged with the attempted capital murder of Deputy Sheriff Gomez.[38]

Douglas Calaway was the first to stand trial for Runyon's murder. The two sheriff's deputies testified that after the Calaway brothers answered Deputy Constable Runyon's knocking on the front door, they heard a round being chambered in a weapon. They quickly stepped off the porch and drew their weapons. They observed a flashlight shining in Runyon's face, and as he tried to push it away, he was dragged into the house and a shot was fired. Defendant Douglas Calaway testified that Runyon had pushed his way into the house, struggled for the gun, and it accidentally went off, killing the deputy constable. Runyon was shot with a .22-caliber pistol containing ratshot, similar to one of the shots fired into Constable Sendejo in Duval County. While that round only wounded Sendejo, Deputy Constable Runyon was shot at close range with the pistol, and the small shot entered his body and destroyed the heart, killing him instantly. Surprisingly, the jury found Douglas Calaway not guilty of murder and released him.[39]

Stephen Calaway was tried six months later and also found not guilty in the murder of Deputy Constable Patrick Runyon. The foreman of the jury, Rick Hebner, stated after the trial, "The fact that the boy came to the door with a .22-caliber pistol, when he had many other guns with larger caliber available to him, indicated to us that he didn't have murder in mind."[40]

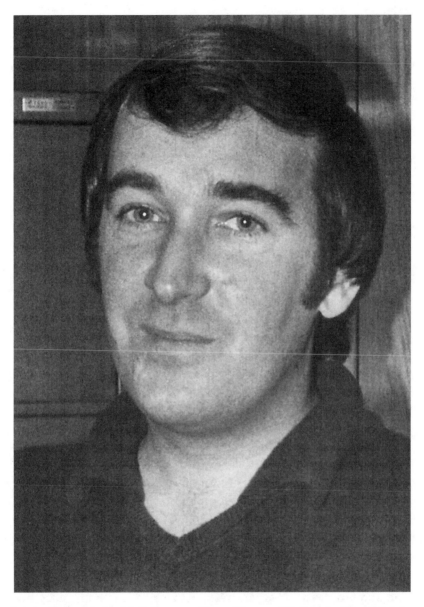

Deputy Constable Patrick S. Runyon, Nueces County, killed in the line of duty in Annaville on February 7, 1981 (courtesy Constable Jim Masur, Precinct No. 6, Nueces County).

Polk County

For almost twenty-five years Bill Garsee had been and was still a sometime professional rodeo clown. Garsee was good enough to work the best known rodeos in Texas, including the famous Prison Rodeo at Huntsville. In 1977, he asked for and was appointed to the vacant job of constable, Precinct No. 3 in Polk County. At fifty-four years of age, but still in good physical shape, Garsee knew that someday he would have to do something besides dodge bulls, and save cowboys from serious injuries. He liked the idea of being a constable, because like clowns in a rodeo, constables also could help people.[41]

Garsee was paid just one dollar a year as constable, so it wasn't the money that drew him into law enforcement, rather Garsee cared deeply for his community. In rural East Texas, lots of people got mixed up in crime mainly because no one cared. In addition to working as a rodeo clown and constable, Bill Garsee worked with the Citizens State Bank in nearby Corrigan as a collection and repossession officer, and as a hand on a number of farms and ranches around his home in Moscow. Garsee had one son from a former marriage, Billy Gene Garsee, who also had worked as a rodeo clown. In 1948, Bill Sr. married Teenie Scarborough, with whom he had two daughters, Brenda and Vickie.[42]

Moscow, Texas, is now no more than a wide spot in the road on Highway 59. Those entering Moscow from the south (from the direction of Livingston, the county seat) are greeted by the sign Have You Seen the Dinosaur? Just beside the sign is a fifteen-foot high dinosaur model. Almost all that is left of the town of Moscow is an older Phillips gasoline station and convenience store housed in a large metal building maybe a hundred yards past the dinosaur, and after that the store and restaurant owned by Garsee's brother A. J. and his wife. At the north end of town is a well-kept rest area with a large metal plaque announcing that William "Bill" Hobby who was managing editor of the *Houston Post* newspaper, Lieutenant Governor, and Governor of Texas, was born in Moscow. Four miles west of Moscow is the boyhood home of John Wesley Hardin, America's most infamous *pistolero*.

Garsee and his wife, Teenie, lived in a modest brick home behind the Phillips station, and it was here on the afternoon of April 7, 1984, that an unidentified man drove his pickup slowly toward the house. Teenie had just come home from nearby Lufkin, and had seen a late-model, blue and silver Chevrolet pickup come toward their house as she parked her car. She had not paid too much attention to the driver, but ran inside to clean up, thinking the driver was probably coming to see Garsee, and might come to the house for coffee. We know that the pickup slowed, then drove into a narrow service road next to the Garsee home, and then a little farther on toward Garsee, who was feeding his horse and dogs near the barn behind his home. The driver stopped, opened his pickup door, stepped out, and from about half a car length away, shot Constable Garsee three times in the chest.[43]

Bill Garsee was dead before anyone could reach him. According to witnesses, his killer stepped back into the vehicle, put the pickup in reverse, and after pulling back out onto the service road, slowly drove away north, unrecognized by several people who had heard the shots and looked outside. Others just a short distance away paid little attention to the shots, for this was rural Texas, and a gun being fired in the neighborhood at a fox or a rabbit was not all that unusual.

Teenie heard the shots, but was confused as to where they had come from. Almost immediately, however, a neighbor pounded on the door shouting that her husband had been shot, and to call the police. Teenie ran to the telephone, called the operator, screamed that her husband had been shot, and ran outside to find him lying dead on the ground.[44]

At least three people near the Garsee home had seen the pickup truck driven by the murderer, but because of its tinted windows, no one could describe the driver, nor had anyone taken notice of the license number. Although at least one similar pickup was stopped that evening, no suspects were detained or arrested in the first twenty-four hours after the murder. There was no apparent motive for the shooting.

Over the next few months, the Texas Rangers were called in, as is normal when small law enforcement departments in Texas have murders to solve. Ranger Tommy Walker out of Livingston was assigned to the case. Composite drawings were published based on descriptions from people who had seen a man asking about a Bill Garsee the day of the murder.[45]

The citizens of northern Polk County, led by the Garsee family, the Moscow-Corrigan Trail Riders Association, and the Citizens State Bank in Corrigan, organized and offered a $17,500 reward for

Constable Bill Garsee, Polk County, Texas, assassinated by unknown person in Moscow, Texas, on April 1, 1984 (courtesy of Teenie Garsee).

information leading to the arrest and conviction of those responsible for the murder. Investigator Charles Staton of the Polk County Sheriff's Department was put in charge of the investigation.

A number of leads took investigators to Michigan, Georgia, and several areas in Texas. As time went on, almost a dozen people were asked and agreed to take polygraph tests, to check parts of their recollections about the murder. Still, no suspects and no confirmed motive for the murder of Constable Bill Garsee have been determined.[46]

Many of the participants participated in interviews for this book: Teenie Garsee; Anthony Page, president of Citizens State Bank where Bill was a sometime collector of overdue bills for the bank; Texas Ranger Don Morris; John Clifton who owned the Chevrolet dealership where Garsee worked on repossessions; A. J. Garsee, Bill's brother; and Chuck Staton, who is now investigator for the district attorney's office in Livingston.

These conversations revealed the following: On Saturday morning, April 7, 1984, Bill Garsee had helped Jeff Westerman with his cattle and then went to Ken Yarborough's ranch to work his cattle. Around noon that same day, an unidentified white male was in San Augustine, some seventy-eight miles northeast of Moscow, asking the whereabouts of "a Bill Garsee, who used to be a rodeo clown." This man, estimated to be about forty-five to fifty years old at the time, was 5'8" to 5'10" in height, about 170 pounds, and wore a gray, suit-type jacket. He asked several people, including Sherry Elumbough, about the Garsee family. Sherry told him she knew the name, but didn't know if the Garsees still lived around San Augustine.[47]

About 2:00 P.M. that afternoon, about the same time Teenie Garsee drove away from Moscow to shop and see friends and family in Lufkin, that same man presumably visited Glady's Cafe in San Augustine, and asked Lillian Steptoe about Bill Garsee. Lillian says she remembers saying she knew the name, but was uncertain about anything else she said. At approximately 4:45 P.M., a man answering the same description showed up at the Gulf gasoline station in Corrigan, just a few miles north of Moscow, and asked for a telephone book. After looking in the book, he appeared very upset, threw the book down and asked about the location of Bill Garsee's house. A local man was getting gas at the time, and told him where Bill lived.[48]

It was only about an hour later that an unidentified white man shot Constable Garsee in back of his home in Moscow. If Bill Garsee knew his killer, he must not have been worried, for he made no

Bill Garsee murder scene in Moscow. Garsee was feeding his animals outside of the barn, when an un-known assassin drove down this road, stopped, shot, and killed Constable Garsee. The assassin then drove off down the small road making his escape (photo by the author).

attempt to reach his gun which was only a few yards away in his pickup. Although the murder was rigorously investigated, no one has ever been arrested.[49]

Some suspect that Garsee must have made someone mad when he repossessed their car, or in some confrontation when he was working as a constable. Some have speculated that Bill Garsee was shot by mistake, that the killer may have been after his son, Billy. Others believe Constable Garsee had discovered someone mixed up in the narcotics trade and was killed before he could report it.

Garsee's murder was not included in the FBI analysis of law-enforcement officers killed in line of duty in 1984, although the case was then, and is today, still unsolved. Constable Bill Garsee's killer can never rest, or quit looking over his shoulder, for there is no statute of limitations for a murderer. The case is forever open.

Travis County

For several days, Chief Deputy Constable David E. Nelson of Precinct No. 3 in Travis County had attempted to serve some civil papers near Lake Travis, outside of Austin. Nelson was always just a little late in finding the person he was attempting to serve, but in the middle of May 1985, he got up very early in the morning and headed for Lake Travis along Lamar Street.[50]

Lamar Street in 1985 was a narrow, congested major road in southwest Austin, and was the main access into Austin from Highway 290. Numerous trucks and travelers heading for southwest Texas and the Hill Country, plus those heading for work in the Austin area, clogged the street early that morning. More than a decade later, Lamar Street at rush hour is still no fun to drive. It must have been especially frustrating to Chief Deputy Constable Nelson, as he no doubt imagined the defendant again driving away just before he arrived. Nelson was driving south along Lamar when suddenly a large flatbed truck backed out of a parking lot near the Oak Hill and Lamar intersections. For whatever reason, Nelson did not react fast enough, and drove into the rear end of the large truck. He died twenty-one days later.[51]

Nacogdoches County

Darrell Lunsford was a big man by many standards. He stood six foot, five inches tall and weighed close to three hundred pounds. He was also someone who went out of his way to help people. His size and his habit of helping people went a long way toward getting him appointed constable in 1983 when the official who held the job decided to retire early. Justice of the peace in Precinct No. 3, Harold Bogue, backed Lunsford for the position. Constable Lunsford thought enough of the job to buy his own patrol car and weapons, and some other equipment was donated by local citizens.[52]

Like many constables in Texas, Lunsford moonlighted. During most days, he was in his own auto parts and repair shop located in Garrison. After he finished work there, he started his second job as constable of Precinct No. 3 in Nacogdoches County, a position he held from 1984 to 1991.[53]

Like much of rural Texas, Precinct No. 3 in Nacogdoches County is not a high crime area. It does have one thing, however, that makes some rural counties in Texas more prone to certain types of crimes than other rural counties. A major highway runs through the center of the county, bringing all sorts of employment opportunities as well as all sorts of problems. Highway 59 is not an Interstate Highway. Although it is mostly a divided four-lane highway that runs from Laredo through Houston and Texarkana before winding its way to Minnesota, there are few luxury hotels, even fewer fancy restaurants, and as it winds its way through East Texas there are few attractions worth stopping to see. Mostly it passes within a hundred feet of thousands of small, rundown houses, mobile-home sales lots, older gasoline stations, and millions of acres of tall trees.

Large trucks make up a major portion of its traffic, but Highway 59 is perhaps best known as a major artery for transporting illegal narcotics from the Texas-Mexican border or from Houston's ship channel to most points north. Unfortunately for Constable Lunsford, Highway 59 is also where he spent much of his time patrolling.

Equally unfortunate is that Constable Lunsford's energy, dedication, and opportunity to serve initially surpassed his training in law enforcement. It was not until September 1985 that constables in Texas were required to obtain approved law-enforcement training and pass a state test either before or during their first two years in office. Consequently, Lunsford's early career as a constable was not always productive. Some cases were thrown out; others were lost in court. But Constable Lunsford also often succeeded. He spent his early years as constable learning the law, getting to know his precinct and his constituents, keeping the peace, ticketing an occasional speeding car, and getting horses, cattle, and an occasional teenager off the road and back home. The voters of Precinct No. 3 liked and respected Darrell Lunsford. T. M. Peterson, a deputy constable who sometimes rode with him on patrol in the later years, said Lunsford "was a fine man, a good peace officer, and loved his work." Apparently Lunsford's constituents thought so, too, reelecting him in 1985 and again in 1989.[54]

It didn't take Lunsford long to realize that many of the cars and trucks he stopped for traffic offenses were carrying narcotics, but because of the cases he had lost in court, he knew he needed help to make good legal narcotics interdiction stops on the highway. There was no money in his early budgets to employ a deputy. Moreover, Constable Lunsford, like many in rural Texas, was a loner. He thought he solved many of his problems by adding a video camera to his patrol car, and using the videotape to help make his cases. This method has proven effective for law-enforcement agencies throughout the state of Texas in many DWI and other cases.[55]

Seven years' experience as constable, some successful seizures of narcotics on Highway 59, completion of several law-enforcement training courses, a strong desire to get the drug dealers off the road, and the video camera in his patrol car worked miracles for Darrell Lunsford. By 1990, he had become an effective force against the transportation of narcotics through East Texas. He had made numerous traffic stops and—thanks to what appeared to be an allergic reaction—detected hundreds of pounds of marijuana, merely by putting his head partially through an open window or by opening a trunk. The videocamera secured in his patrol car confirmed probable cause for initially stopping the vehicle and recorded his discoveries.[56]

Working narcotics interdiction alone, at night, on a lonely and dark highway, even with a videocamera running, is something that many law-enforcement agencies will not approve. But regardless of the obvious danger, someplace in Texas it happens almost every night, because few law-enforcement budgets allow for more than one officer in a vehicle. Lunsford recognized the risks he was taking and actually told his friend Justice Harold Bogue, "If anything ever happens to me, you will be able to see it on the camera." But the risk did not stop his efforts to catch more drug dealers.[57]

On January 23, 1991, at 1:25 A.M., Lunsford was about finished patrolling and was almost home in Garrison when the car in front of him swerved several times across the yellow center line. Lunsford, suspecting he was behind a drinking driver, turned on his overhead lights and his videocamera. By either design or accident he pulled the vehicle over on the side of the road directly across Highway 59 from the front door of his auto parts shop. Constable Lunsford picked up the microphone of his radio, and reported the traffic stop, gave the license number of the car stopped, and opened his car door. As Lunsford exited his patrol car and started forward, the driver of the stopped car, twenty-four-year-old Reynaldo Villareal, opened the door and walked toward Lunsford. They met about halfway and Constable Lunsford asked for his driver's license. Villareal admitted he had no license with him, but told Lunsford he was only helping drive his brother, Baldemar, who had recently come to visit, and a friend to a possible job they knew about in faraway Maine.[58]

He went forward to talk to the brother, who changed the story somewhat by claiming to have been in Texas for a month. Constable Lunsford noted a third passenger in the car, and did what was by now normal procedure for him. That was to ask for permission to look in the trunk. Some time during the traffic stop, a patrol car from the Nacogdoches Sheriff's Department drove past Constable Lunsford, saw what was going on, and drove away on patrol. If Lunsford noticed the other police car drive away, it probably didn't surprise him, for he did not always see eye to eye with that department and there was little cooperation with his agency.[59]

Baldemar stepped out of the stopped car as the trunk was opened. Even on the wintry night, Lunsford most likely reacted to the smell, reached in and opened a duffle bag later found to contain some forty pounds of marijuana. As Lunsford turned away from the vehicle trunk and toward the two occupants, he was jumped by the two men, one grabbing him around his hips and legs, the other grabbing at his arms. Constable Lunsford was forty-seven years old and stood a foot taller than his assailants, but there were just too many hands to ward off successfully. The other passenger quickly got out of the car, and suddenly there were three against one. Lunsford's legs were pulled out from under him, and he fell to the ground, losing all the advantage his size offered. They rolled into the ditch, and one man kicked him in the head.[60]

One of the hands pulled Lunsford's pistol from its holster, shoved it against his neck, and with one shot severed his spinal cord. The fight was over, and Constable Lunsford was dead. The three

Highway 59, Garrison, Texas. Constable Darrell Lunsford was murdered during a traffic stop about fifty yards down Highway 59 from where this photo was taken, nearly opposite his auto repair shop and sign (photo by author).

criminals took his gun, badge, and wallet; jumped into their car; and sped away.[61]

What happened next was the luckiest thing possible for those in law enforcement. Instead of speeding out of Texas, the killers panicked, drove only a relatively short distance to a nearby side road, abandoned the car, and ran off into the thick woods surrounding Corrigan. What the killers did not know was just what Lunsford had told his friend Judge Bogue months before. The videocamera in the patrol car had recorded all of the action, and the film would identify all three of the killers.[62]

Reynaldo Villareal was captured the next afternoon near Garrison when he looked up the business end of a shotgun held by a man whose wife recognized the man she saw walking down their road as the same person she had seen on a televised copy of Lunsford's tape. Baldemar Villareal was captured the next day walking down nearby railway tracks, and Jesse Zambrano was caught a week later when he showed up outside a nearby grocery store.[63]

Constable Darrell Lunsford burns illegal drugs. Following the seizure of several marijuana plants in the trunk of a vehicle on Highway 59 by Constable Lunsford, officers were led to the area where the plants were harvested (courtesy Shirley Lunsford, wife of Darrell Lunsford).

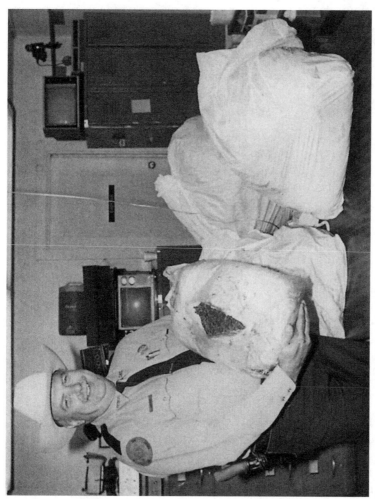

Constable Darrell Lunsford, Nacogdoches County, Texas, with over three hundred pounds of marijuana he seized during a traffic stop on Highway 59, Nacogdoches County (courtesy Shirley Lunsford, wife of Darrell Lunsford).

To many, it seemed like a "slam-dunk" prosecution: establish the probable cause of the vehicle stop, then just play the videotape recovered from Darrell's vehicle showing the murder, and rest the case. For some reason, the case was transferred from state district court to federal court jurisdiction. A federal attorney in Tyler failed to prove an element of the prosecution's case and, as a result, no death sentence was possible, even with a video showing the murder. Jesse Zambrano was sentenced to thirty years and Reynaldo Villareal thirty-five years in prison. The man who pulled the trigger, Baldemar Villareal, received a life sentence.[64]

Jasper County

Roy V. Richardson was elected constable in Precinct No. 5, in Jasper County, in late 1993. At 8:17 P.M. on Tuesday, January 9, 1996, Constable Richardson was driving west on Farm Road 1007, about ten miles north of the town of Jasper, when he approached U.S. Highway 96 and stopped at a stop sign on an unlighted section of the highway. He then pulled out into the highway, but failed to yield the right-of-way to an oncoming tractor-trailer truck. The truck, although it attempted to avoid a collision, struck Richardson's vehicle, fatally injuring Constable Richardson, who died on January 17, 1996.[65]

Harris County

On the night of September 29, 1998, Deputy Constable Ray Leo "Michael" Eakin III was on duty in northern Harris County. Michael, as he preferred to be called, had served in Harris County's Precinct No. 1 for about three years and before that had worked about two years in law enforcement in Montgomery County. About 1:00 A.M. he was patrolling the area where he had lived as a youngster, before the family had moved away because the neighborhood had become too dangerous. Deputy Eakin stopped a vehicle carrying five men and two women for a minor traffic offense. All but one of the passengers, who said his name was Michael Lopez, were able to present identification.

Eakin returned to his patrol unit to request another unit to assist him, then came back to the stopped vehicle. He asked Lopez to step out of the vehicle for further identification. Lopez got out, but ran away from the scene. Deputy Eakin chased Lopez only a short distance before catching him behind a nearby building. As Eakin struggled to handcuff him, the seventeen-year-old Lopez drew a cheap .38-caliber revolver from his belt, twisted around, and shot Eakin twice in the head, killing him almost instantly.

Lopez fled the scene, but was arrested the next day. He was on juvenile probation at the time of the murder, and confessed that he was afraid that he would be turned over to the Probation Department for punishment. Instead, he chose to murder Deputy Constable Michael Eakin, and he has now been charged with capital murder of a peace officer, which carries a maximum penalty of death by lethal injection. [66]

WHAT MIGHT THE FUTURE HOLD?

Since 1960, in a number of communities in the state of Texas, the office of constable has come under attack both from lawbreakers and from some members of local government. The latter contend that the elected office of constable is no longer necessary or desirable, and tax dollars can be saved by consolidating many county and precinct offices.

In some Texas counties this has made perfect sense to many voters, for they had no idea what a constable does or why the office should or should not continue. Perhaps too few constables take the time to explain their office to the voters. Nonetheless, over the last several decades a number of Texas counties have asked their legislators to propose a constitutional amendment making it possible for individual counties to abolish the office of constable, as well as other county positions. One of the biggest problems with this type of action is that voters in 254 counties then vote on an individual county's initiative, and by sometimes bundling several offices together in one initiative, voters further lose their ability to choose.

An alternative to abolishing the office of constable is to make the office more responsive by having voters pay more attention to those running for the office, and by making their concerns and problems known among candidates for the office. Then one could vote for the most qualified and best informed about precinct law enforcement problems.

Appendix A
Some Constables Outside of Texas

During the first half of the nineteenth century, constables were the dominant law enforcement officer in many counties across the United States. But stories of constables before the Civil War are as rare as stories of sheriffs—they seldom survive except where lives were lost or where a family has documented the exploits of a relative. Since Appomattox, better record keeping and more newspapers have contributed to our knowledge of individual law enforcement officers. This book is not intended to recount in detail the activities of constables throughout the fifty states. But a number of well-known and not so well-known lawmen outside of Texas served as constables during their career. Here are some of their stories.

West of the Mississippi

James Butler Hickok, Constable of Monticello Township, Johnson County, Kansas, 1858

James Butler Hickok was born and reared in Illinois. In June 1856, aged nineteen, he traveled with his brother Lorenzo to the Kansas Territory to search for new opportunities. The Kansas Territory, embroiled in an undeclared war between pro- and antislavery elements, was not a safe place for many settlers in the 1850s. In 1856 or 1857, Hickok joined James H. Lane's Free State Army, an antislavery group. In late 1857, he left the Free State Army for the small community of Monticello, in Johnson County, Kansas, and worked a 160-acre homestead claim.[1]

On March 22, 1858, Hickok, aged twenty, was elected constable of Monticello Township, his first job in law enforcement. During this time, Hickok's letters show him to be a busy constable and an enthusiastic farmer. His own work seems to have been nonviolent.

James Butler "Wild Bill" Hickok (courtesy Kansas State Historical Society).

James Butler "Wild Bill" Hickok, in buckskins with knife and pair of revolvers (courtesy Kansas State Historical Society).

He wrote to his family about his desire for rule of law and less violence in Kansas.[2] About six months later, Hickok resigned and left Monticello, possibly owing to a waning romance and a proslavery raid that burned out his cabin. He spent the next two years as a stagecoach and wagon driver.[3] It would be several years before Hickok would wear another badge.

During this period, James Butler Hickok became "Wild Bill." After serving as a scout, courier, and spy during the Civil War, he lost an election for police chief in Springfield, Missouri, and then was defeated as a candidate for sheriff of Ellsworth County, Kansas. He worked for some time as a scout for Custer's Seventh Cavalry, and then as a deputy U.S. marshal. Finally, in August 1869, Hickok was elected sheriff of Ellis County, Kansas.[4] He had already killed two men, and over the next year, Hickok would kill three more men in Hays City in the line of duty.

In 1871, Hickok was hired as marshal of Abilene, the first trail town of Kansas. While marshal, Hickok killed another man. After accidentally killing his own deputy he never again shot at another man. He died six years later, killed by an assassin's bullet in Deadwood, Dakota Territory on August 2, 1876.

Chauncey Belden Whitney, Constable of Ellsworth County, Kansas, 1867 to 1868

Ellsworth, Kansas, was established in January 1867, only a short time before the Union Pacific Railroad came through. Chauncey Whitney, who had spent his early years as an Indian fighter, arrived in Ellsworth about the same time as the railroad, and became the first constable, and sole law enforcement, in what was to become a major cattle trail town. At the behest of county commissioners, he began in September to enforce licensing, and a month later to build the first jail.[5]

After he left office, Whitney joined a group of civilian scouts organized by Major George A. Forsyth, and took part in the famous fight at Beecher Island, when Roman Nose and several hundred hostile Indians attacked. He continued to fight Indians for several more years,[6] and later served as town marshal of Ellsworth and sheriff of Ellsworth County.[7]

By 1873, the town of Ellsworth had acquired a police force of five. Along with Texas cowboys driving cattle, a number of notorious

Chauncey Belden Whitney, constable, Indian fighter, town marshal, and sheriff of Ellsworth, Kansas, was shot and killed on August 15, 1873 (courtesy Kansas State Historical Society).

gamblers (including Ben and Billy Thompson), drunks, and thugs had drifted into the Ellsworth area. Six homicides had taken place in town. On August 15, Sheriff C. B. Whitney was attempting to calm a confrontation between the police and Texas cowboys, when a drunk Billy Thompson shot and killed Sheriff Whitney. Thompson outran the posse, and did not return for almost four years. Put on trial at that time, Billy Thompson was acquitted of Sheriff Whitney's murder.[8]

Constable Charles Faber, Las Animas, Colorado, 1876

Like many Old West towns, Las Animas, Colorado, had an ordinance against carrying guns inside town limits. Charles Faber was a constable and deputy sheriff in Las Animas. On December 21, 1876, well-known rancher and gunman Clay Allison and his brother John were drinking in a local saloon and ignored Constable Faber when he asked them to check their guns.[9] Both of the Allisons continued to drink until they turned surly. Faber came back to the saloon with two deputies to disarm them. As they entered the saloon, a warning was heard, and Faber shot John Allison. Clay Allison shot Faber, hitting him in the chest. Constable Faber dropped his shotgun, which fired, wounding John Allison again.[10]

When it was over, Faber was dead, John Allison was badly wounded, and the two deputies fled. Clay Allison was arrested by the sheriff, and John Allison was taken to the doctor. As was fairly common in the Old West, both brothers were eventually released without punishment, although Constable Faber had been killed in the line of duty.

W. C. Kelly, Constable of Caldwell, Kansas, 1879 to 1880

W. C. Kelly was a constable in Caldwell, Kansas, at a time when the town was first experiencing life as a new cattle town. On the afternoon of July 7, 1879, Constable W. C. Kelly and Deputy Constable John Wilson heard gunshots from down the street in Caldwell. It quickly became evident that a couple of drunk cowboys, George Wood and Jake Adams,[11] were "taking the town" by shooting it up. Constable Kelly deputized George W. Flatt, and the three lawmen went to the Occidental Saloon to arrest Wood and Adams, but there was a shootout. When it was over, both cowboys were dead and Deputy Wilson was wounded. Flatt's pistol work on the

Loading Texas cattle at a Kansas trail town (courtesy Kansas State Historical Society).

side of law and order assured him the job of town marshal of Caldwell when the town was organized six weeks later, on August 21, 1879. He served as an effective town marshal until April 1880,[12] then was murdered two months later. The murder was never solved.

Constable Dave "Mysterious Dave" Mather, Las Vegas, New Mexico, 1879

Dave Mather, or "Mysterious Dave" as he was called, appeared comfortable on either side of the law. Dave has, from time to time, been identified as a farmer, horse thief, prospector, buffalo hunter, train robber, law officer, and gambler. This type of life was far from unusual in the Old West, and apparently the first thirty-four years of Mysterious Dave's life are really a mystery. In the stories and even a book written about Mather, most of his life before 1879 is a montage of rumor, association, and suppositions, with little documented fact.[13]

The Santa Fe Railway arrived in Las Vegas, New Mexico, on July 1, 1879. Many in New Mexico dreamed of making Las Vegas the major trade center in the territory, including a group of gangsters, who would soon dominate local government. A few months before, Mather was indicted for participating in a train robbery thought to have been committed by this gang. Mather pleaded not guilty, and because prosecution witnesses failed to appear, he was released.[14]

Although Mather appears to have been involved with this group of train robbers and gangsters, he was appointed deputy U.S. marshal in Las Vegas. By late 1879, Mather had also been appointed a constable in Las Vegas, probably to supplement his income.[15] On January 25, 1880, Constable Dave was attempting to stop a gun battle when Joseph Castello threatened Mather, pointing his gun at the constable. Mather drew his own gun, fired one shot, and killed Castello.[16]

After serving as constable, Mather drifted back to Dodge City, Kansas, where in 1883 he was appointed deputy city marshal and deputy sheriff. In February 1884, he ran for city constable, but was defeated. During the first few years after his defeat, Mather was involved in several gunfights and usually came out the winner. But Mysterious Dave remained mysterious to the end. While awaiting trial for a killing in Kansas, he saddled his horse, rode to Nebraska, and permanently faded from view.[17]

"Mysterious Dave," David A. Mather. Photo taken some time during his term as assistant marshal of Dodge City, June 1, 1883, to April 10, 1884 (courtesy Western History Collections, University of Oklahoma Library).

Dodge City Peace Commission, June 7, 1883. Luke Short, owner of the Long Branch Saloon, had run-ins with police in April and May 1883, and asked some old friends for "support." Wyatt Earp (seated, second from left), Bat Masterson (standing third from left next to Luke Short), and the others shown went to Dodge City to show support for their friend Luke Short six days after "Mysterious" Dave Mather became assistant marshal (courtesy Western History Collections, University of Oklahoma Library).

Virgil W. Earp, Constable in Prescott, Arizona Territory, 1878 to 1879, and Colton, California, 1886 to 1887; and Wyatt B. Earp, Constable in Lamar, Missouri, 1870

Virgil Earp was the second of eight children. Wyatt Earp was the fourth, born five years after brother Virgil. They spent most of their childhood moving from state to state, guided by a father, Nicholas Earp, who was always influential in the mostly rural places where he settled. From time to time, Nicholas Earp was a farmer, a constable in Warren County and in Lamar Township, Missouri, justice of the peace, notary public, Mexican War veteran, and an active politician.[18] He and his wife left Illinois for California in May 1864 with five of their children.[19] Virgil Earp fought in the Civil War, spending three years in the 83rd Regiment of Illinois Volunteer Infantry, and mustered out in 1865.

Virgil apparently went to Missouri after he left the army, and spent several years as a freighter and stage driver, not unlike Wild Bill Hickok in his early years. After only four years in California, most of the Earp family began moving back to the Midwest. In the meantime, Virgil met Wyatt in Wyoming and for a brief time they worked for the railroad. James and Morgan drifted to Montana. Nicholas and other family members came to the little settlement of Lamar, in Barton County, Missouri, in 1869. The rest of his family soon followed.

Soon after arrival in Lamar, Nicholas was appointed town constable, but he resigned that position a few months later to work as justice of the peace. It was here, not long after his arrival, that Wyatt Earp married his first wife, Urilla Sutherland on January 10, 1870. A few months later, Wyatt Earp replaced his father as town constable, the first of many law enforcement jobs he would hold. Four months after that, Virgil Earp and seventeen-year-old Rosella Dragoo, who had accompanied the Earp family to Lamar, were married. This was Virgil's second wife.[20]

Wyatt Earp's tenure as constable of the rural township of Lamar, Missouri, appeared peaceful enough, with the only record of his activity being a question whether he would be required to round up stray hogs in the town, and the jailing of several drunks. Wyatt appeared satisfied with this job, for he was elected town constable in

Nicholas P. Earp with second wife Virginia Ann Cooksie. Nicholas was patriarch of the Earp family, a sometime attorney, justice of the peace, farmer, constable, Mexican War veteran, notary public, and politician (courtesy Kansas State Historical Society).

November 1870, by a vote of 137 to 108, defeating his half-brother Newton. Two other candidates drew a total of forty-three votes.[21]

Just a few months later, Urilla Earp died in childbirth, along with the baby. Virgil's wife Rosella disappeared from history about the same time; it has been suggested that she died or was kidnapped by her disgruntled family, who left Missouri telling no one of their destination. In 1873, Virgil took a third wife, Alvira, or "Allie" Sullivan, and although there is no record of marriage, they stayed together until his death thirty years later.[22]

In 1874, Wyatt Earp moved to Wichita, Kansas, where he served for several months as a policeman. After being dismissed from that job, he drifted to Dodge City, where he made his name as a lawman. The remainder of the Earp family, including Nicholas, Newton, Virgil and Allie, left Missouri in 1876 and proceeded west, again with California as their ultimate destination.

Virgil and Allie left the group in Prescott, the capital of Arizona Territory, and spent most of 1877 to 1879 in that area. At first Virgil helped deliver the U.S. mail on a rural route. Then in October 1877, he was part of a posse called to assist Constable Frank Murray in arresting two bandits who had been recognized in Prescott. The two were killed in a shootout with the law, which included a hastily deputized Virgil Earp. In 1878, Virgil was employed as night watchman in Prescott, and in November of that year was elected constable of Prescott Precinct, with 386 votes. He resigned the night watchman position. As with most constables at the time, the monthly salary was supplemented by fees earned when delivering papers (summonses, citations, and warrants), transporting prisoners, collecting taxes, issuing licenses to saloons or prostitutes, and a percentage of sales of seized property.[23]

In addition to the above, Constable Virgil Earp was involved in day-to-day law enforcement duties. It is interesting to note that he faced problems in 1879 Arizona that constables throughout the United States, including Texas, still face more than a hundred years later. He was sued in 1879 for seizing and selling property that was not subject to seizure, and was fined $85.00.[24]

In 1879, James, Wyatt, Morgan, and Virgil and their wives moved to Tombstone, Arizona, with dreams of owning mines and saloons, running stage lines, and participating in other money-making schemes in a boomtown. While in Tombstone, Wyatt was appointed deputy marshal and Virgil was appointed town marshal.

Virgil Earp was constable in Prescott, Arizona, and Colton, California (courtesy Western History Collections, University of Oklahoma Library).

Wyatt Earp in his twenties, Dodge City, Kansas (courtesy Kansas State Historical Society).

Wyatt's law enforcement duties brought him in contact with at least one other constable, who has added to the mystique that Wyatt worked so hard to develop. On January 14, 1881, while Wyatt was serving as a deputy U.S. marshal in Tombstone, Constable George McKelvey arrested John O'Rourke, "Johnny-Behind-the-Deuce," a professional gambler, for the murder of popular mining engineer Henry Schneider. Constable McKelvey transported O'Rourke to the jail in Tombstone, and it was there that the myth of Wyatt Earp holding off a lynch mob was born. In fact, Earp and several other lawmen pushed O'Rourke into a wagon, and transported him to safety in Tucson when they got word that a lynch mob was forming.[25]

A few months later, on October 26, 1881, town marshal Virgil Earp, his brothers Morgan and Wyatt, and Doc Holliday were involved in the OK Corral shootout, and Virgil was wounded in the leg. On December 28, just before midnight, Virgil was ambushed on the streets of Tombstone. He suffered another serious gunshot wound in his left arm and back. He lost four inches of bone from the arm, leaving it stiff and almost useless.[26]

In March 1882, Morgan Earp was killed, shot in the back while playing pool. All the remaining Earps except Wyatt and his younger brother Warren headed to California. On July 2, 1886, Virgil Earp was elected constable of the village of Colton, California, a major rail junction located east of Los Angeles, where Nicholas Earp was justice of the peace. The people of Colton must have been very comfortable with Virgil Earp as their constable, for in July 1887, the Village of Colton incorporated, and elected him as their new city marshal. He won the job with 116 to 57 votes. In 1889, Virgil Earp resigned as city marshal of Colton, moving eventually to Nevada, where he died in 1905.[27]

A drifter to the end, Wyatt eventually left Arizona, traveled throughout the West and died in Los Angeles in 1929.

EAST OF THE MISSISSIPPI

During the late nineteenth century, the federal government and some state governments east of the Mississippi tried to tax the making and selling of whiskey. This ignited a war with moonshiners that lasted from the late 1870s to the 1930s. Federal Internal Revenue agents, U.S. marshals, and occasionally regular army troops hunted the illegal whiskey makers in many remote parts of the southern states, especially North and South Carolina, Georgia, Mississippi, and Louisiana.

Unlike Texas with its system of precinct and county constables, South Carolina has state constables. This system allows these peace officers to perform their duty anywhere within the state without jurisdictional problems. In 1892, the state of South Carolina, with federal assistance, aggressively set out to destroy or confiscate untaxed, illegally made moonshine whiskey. To do this, the state constables were authorized to obtain warrants to search any place they suspected such illegal whiskey was stored. This law made state constables and federal agents the target of any moonshiner. The state of South Carolina repealed many of its laws affecting illegal whiskey in 1907. Just a decade later, however, in 1919, the Volstead Law again ignited the war against moonshiners.[28]

The period from 1920 to 1940 was also apparently a good time to kill constables and other peace officers in the United States. Contrary to the popular wisdom, according to data from the National Law Enforcement Officers Memorial, more constables from across the United States were killed in the line of duty from 1920 to 1940 than during the following sixty years. Furthermore, for all the stories, myths, and romances written about lawmen dying in the Old West, more constables from across the United States are confirmed killed in the line of duty during these same twenty years than are known to have been killed during the fifty years between 1870 to 1920. These numbers may be the result of a lack of record keeping in the years before this century, but they do represent the current statistics available.[29]

These statistics, however, are not true of Texas constables. Of the twenty-five confirmed deaths in line of duty since 1900 for Texas constables and deputy constables, eight, or thirty-three percent, were killed in the 1970s, and approximately seventy percent of those killed were murdered since 1961. These are probably fairly reliable numbers for this century; however, since no Texas constables are officially listed in the National Memorial as having been killed in the line of duty before 1910, and we know there were some, we may never have an accurate estimate of overall constable deaths.[30]

James H. Howard, State Constable, South Carolina, 1924

On January 31, 1924, a group of law enforcement officers, including two federal prohibition agents and one state constable, were searching a rough area for an illegal whiskey still near Hogback Mountain, in Greenville County, South Carolina. State Constable James Holland Howard was a member of the group.

James Howard was not an outsider, as the federal agents were; however, he was just as hated and feared by the moonshiners. The Howard family had lived in this area of South Carolina for over 150 years, and Howard's great-grandfather was a well known hero of the Revolutionary War. His family had also had a number of scrapes with the law over illegal stills in the distant past, but Constable Howard was so convinced that moonshine alcohol was the "curse of the mountains" that he had volunteered for the raid.[31]

James Howard was well known and highly regarded by law enforcement agencies in the Greenville area, and that day had even brought his son, Clarence, along on the raid. Constable Howard recognized the danger he placed himself in, and it was known he was hated as a traitor by the whiskey makers. As expressed by Dr. William Wilbanks, who has compiled an excellent book on officers killed in the line of duty in Greenville County, Howard's "devotion to the task and bravery were exceptional."

As the group of law-enforcement officers moved up the mountain toward the suspected still, they met two men coming down, took a pistol from one of them, and arrested them. A federal agent and James Howard's son were left to guard the men. Federal Agent Ruben Gosnell and State Constable James Howard climbed to the site of the still and separated to make sure no moonshiners escaped. A few minutes later Agent Gosnell heard shots, and two men ran by him. He chased one, Holland Pittman, who when captured had an unfired pistol, but the other man escaped. When Agent Gosnell and his prisoner returned to the still they found James Howard dead, shot five times in the body. One shot had entered from the front, and the others had been shot into his back, probably as he lay wounded.[32]

Holland Pittman's father, Alexander Pittman, surrendered the next day and was charged with the murder of Constable Howard. A coroner's jury refused to fix the responsibility for the death of

Constable Howard on the Pittmans, but the solicitor (district attorney) pursued prosecution. Howard and Alexander Pittman were tried for the murder, and after deliberating only forty minutes, the jury returned a verdict of guilty, with a death sentence. On appeal the guilty verdict was upheld by the South Carolina Supreme Court, but the death sentence was commuted to life for both men. In 1933, barely nine years after murdering Constable Howard, both men were paroled and just eighteen months later they were pardoned by the governor.[33]

John Edward Dickson, Deputy Constable of District 2, Dade County, Florida, 1932 to 1933

Just two months after Alexander and Howard Pittman were paroled in South Carolina for the cold-blooded murder of Constable Howard, Florida Deputy Constable John Edward Dickson was shot and killed in Dade County, and Constable Charles Dillon was wounded in the process of carrying out a court-ordered eviction, often a very dangerous act and one disliked by many constables. The killer, Reedy Corker, was captured, but for some reason was not indicted by a Dade County grand jury. It has been speculated that the grand jury voted against indictment because of the unpopularity of evictions during the Great Depression, and also because of its timing, on Christmas Eve. No one was ever tried for the murder of Deputy Constable John Dickson.[34]

Luther T. Hardison, Constable, Coral Gables, Florida, 1948 to 1951

It is not unusual even today for constables to transport prisoners for various law enforcement agencies, because they often have a more flexible schedule than other agents. Hired in 1925, Luther Hardison was the first police officer in Coconut Grove, Florida, and at various times he served as a Miami police officer and as deputy sheriff in Collier and Dade Counties. In 1948, having been a peace officer for almost twenty-five years, he was elected constable of District 3, Dade County, Florida.[35]

On February 2, 1951, twenty-two-year-old Harris Mullis walked into a police station in Los Angeles and confessed to a burglary and auto theft in Coral Gables, Florida. As constable of District 3, which included Coral Gables, Luther Hardison decided to travel to

California and bring Mullis back to Florida. Hardison picked up the prisoner in Los Angeles, but for some reason decided not to use handcuffs or leg-irons on Mullis for the long cross-country trip back to Florida. The decision was not a wise one.

At about 1:00 A.M. on February 17, 1951, near Mobile, Alabama, Mullis shot and killed Constable Hardison with a gun Hardison had hidden under the front seat. He then dumped the body and drove west to Fort Worth, where he abandoned the constable's car. The killing created immense national publicity, and seven days later Mullis was captured in New York City.[36]

Mullis was tried for murder and received a death sentence, but Florida Governor Gordon Parsons commuted the death sentence to life in prison. Over the next thirty-seven years Mullis was paroled three times (once in 1968 and twice in 1970), only to violate parole each time and be returned to prison. He also escaped from prison four times (1974, 1976, 1979, and 1980), but was recaptured each time. Harris Mullis finally died in prison in 1988.[37]

Buford H. Pusser, Constable of District 3, McNary County, Tennessee, 1962 to 1964 and 1970 to 1974

Buford Pusser was born in McNary County, Tennessee, in 1937, and spent all of his life there except for a brief tour of duty in the U.S. Marines (he received a medical discharge) and about five years working in Chicago. McNary County is located on the Mississippi-Tennessee state line, and it was in this corrupt area that Pusser would make his reputation.

Pusser claims that on his first visit in 1954 to the state line he saw Louise Hathcock beat a sailor to death with a claw hammer at the White Iris Club. Louise, one of the club's owners, was said to have told a deputy sheriff that the sailor had died of a heart attack, and the deputy said, "All right, Louise, if you say so. Get me a drink while I call an ambulance." Louise was married to Jack Hathcock, who had organized the State-Line Mob, which controlled gambling, illegal whiskey, and prostitution in the area.[38]

Jack Hathcock was a local boy, whose forty-acre family farm was in McNary County. It is said that he earned his spending money as a boy by selling moonshine whiskey to schoolmates at Michie Elementary School. Later, Jack decided the easiest money was in the state-line clubs and moonshine whiskey. Hathcock was managing one of these clubs when he met and married Louise Anderson from Alcorn County, Mississippi.[39]

Pusser's next visit to the state line was in 1957, when he won over a hundred dollars in a dice game at the Plantation Club, owned by the Hathcocks, in Mississippi. But instead of enjoying his winnings, he had to have 192 stitches in his head and face, to close the wounds he received when four men beat him up outside the club and robbed him of his money. Buford left for Chicago, where he found better jobs and a wife; he swore he would get even.

His promise of revenge must have crossed state lines, for in early 1960, Pusser and two friends in Chicago were suddenly arrested on warrants out of Alcorn County, Mississippi. They were charged with armed robbery and attempted murder of Jack Hathcock. The trial was short. The prosecuting attorney claimed Pusser had tried to get even for his beating at the club in 1957; however, Buford and his two friends were able to show their time cards from the Union Bag Company in Chicago, proving they had been at work when the robbery happened, so they were released.

Two years later, in 1962, Pusser and family found themselves in McNary County, Tennessee, where his father was chief of police in tiny Adamsville.[40] Shortly after their arrival, his father resigned and requested that Buford be appointed to the position. The twenty-four-year-old was now police chief, and in September that same year, he also decided to run for constable of District 3. He won the election. Two years later, Pusser ran for sheriff of McNary County, Tennessee as a Republican. During the campaign Jack Hathcock was murdered. Louise Hathcock was charged with the murder, but was "no-billed" by the grand jury. Pusser won the sheriff's race by less than 250 votes out of just over sixty-three hundred votes cast.[41]

Almost from his first day in office, Sheriff Pusser was at war with the State-Line Mob and moonshiners. In his first term as sheriff, he raided over a hundred illegal stills in Tennessee and arrested almost twice that many people for possession of illegal whiskey. Twice during his first term, he was attacked and wounded, but his closest brush with death came when he went to arrest Louise Hathcock for possession of illegal whiskey and theft. Louise was drunk when Pusser and his deputies arrived. She asked to speak to him privately in her office, but when they walked through the door, she pulled a gun and shot at him. She missed, and aimed a second time at Pusser's head, and the gun misfired. She never pulled the trigger the third time, for by then Pusser had shot her three times with his .41-caliber magnum pistol, and she fell dead on the floor.[42]

Early on Saturday morning, August 12, 1967, Sheriff Pusser was awakened by an anonymous telephone call, asking for his help in preventing a fight and keeping the peace. This was pretty ordinary stuff, and similar calls had pulled Pusser out of bed on a number of other nights. The fight was supposed to take place on one of McNary County's lonely country roads. Buford's wife, Pauline, asked to go with him. As they approached the site, a black car pulled up alongside them and fired into their car. In only a few minutes, Pauline lay dead in the front seat, shot twice in the head, and Buford Pusser was severely wounded. Investigators would later count eleven bullet holes in the sheriff's car. Although severely wounded, with his lower jaw shot away, Pusser had survived another attempt on his life. His wife was buried near their home.[43]

In 1970, at the end of his third two-year term, Pusser could no longer run for sheriff in Tennessee, so he again ran for constable in District 3, and won with eighty-four write-in votes. A movie about his life, *Walking Tall*, and national recognition for cleaning up the State-Line Mob came to Pusser between 1970 and 1974. Another movie was being planned when he was killed in a single-car accident on August 21, 1974. Pusser was thirty-six years old when he died.[44]

Valdon A. Keith, State Constable of South Carolina, 1982 to 1985

Valdon Keith was a qualified state constable, which provided him with law enforcement jurisdiction throughout the state of South Carolina. Deputy sheriffs in South Carolina were often glad to have a state constable riding with them, as it extended their jurisdiction outside their county when necessary.

On November 28, 1985, Thanksgiving morning, Samuel Leroy Wodke and Wilber Rutledge Corvette robbed the Family Mart in Greenville, South Carolina. Wodke carried a machine gun, while Corvette was armed with a semiautomatic pistol. They drove away with about ten thousand dollars in cash and food stamps in a car driven by Wodke's son, Richard. A witness to the robbery followed them and informed the police of their description and direction of travel.[45]

Two Greenville County deputy sheriffs quickly spotted the three fugitives, and a chase began. State Constable Valdon Keith was riding with Deputy Sheriff Dennis Eubanks in one of the patrol cars. In an effort to box the fugitives in, they pulled up beside them, but the fugitives dodged into a parking lot and sprayed the patrol car with bullets. Constable Keith was hit in the head, and the perpetrators fled the scene. Paramedics declared Valdon Keith dead soon after.[46]

Twelve hours later in nearby Gaston, South Carolina, the fugitives' vehicle was located in the yard of the people who had loaned it earlier to Wodke and Corvette. A manhunt followed, and all three were quickly arrested. Samuel Wodke, forty, was the murderer of Constable Keith, and was on intensive parole at the time of the murder, serving a twenty-year sentence for a previous armed robbery. Wilber Corvette, thirty-two, was also on parole, having been convicted of a narcotics and racketeering offense.[47]

Both were found guilty. The judge sentenced Samuel Wodke to life plus twenty-five years, and later Corvette was sentenced to twenty-one years. Richard Wodke received a ten-year suspended sentence and intensive parole for five years. Wilber Corvette was recently released from prison, and in 1994, Samuel Wodke escaped from prison, only to be captured in March 1996 in Morgan City, after being featured on the TV program *Unsolved Mysteries*.

APPENDIX B

A Look at Today's Constables

Duties and Responsibilities of Modern Constables

Regardless of changes in its administrative nature, the office of constable has been authorized in every Texas constitution since the days of the Republic, but it is in the Texas Code of Criminal Procedure, the Texas Penal Code, the Texas Local Government Code, and other assorted laws, rules, and regulations that the general duties of Texas constables are spelled out in detail. Constables and deputy constables are classified as peace officers by the Texas Code of Criminal Procedures, and only after meeting specified qualifications, equivalent to those for all other peace officers in the state of Texas, are constables licensed by the Texas Commission on Law Enforcement Officer Standards and Education (TCLEOSE).

A new amendment to the Texas Constitution, passed in 1997, requires constables to meet certain qualifications for office that were not enumerated in the Constitution. This amendment is expected to have little impact on this office due to the licensing and mandatory training requirements already in effect since 1985.

By command of Article 2.13 Code of Criminal Procedure, it is the duty of every peace officer to:

1. preserve the peace within the officer's jurisdiction by all lawful means;

2. interfere without warrant to prevent or suppress crime where authorized by the Code of Criminal Procedure;

3. execute all lawful criminal process issued to the officer by any magistrate or court;

199

4. give notice to some magistrate of all offenses committed within the officer's jurisdiction, where the officer has good reason to believe there has been a violation of the penal law;

5. arrest offenders without warrant in every case where the officer is authorized by law, in order that they may be taken before the proper magistrate or court to be tried.[1]

Consequently, to keep the peace, the constable in Texas may perform patrol, enforce traffic regulations, undertake investigations, arrest lawbreakers, carry out execution of judgments, and summon persons to aid him in his duties when necessary and to complete juries. He may seize, impound, and sell real and personal property as directed by law. The constable is also an associate member of the Texas Department of Public Safety.[2]

Although the constable is considered a local precinct officer, his territorial jurisdiction, like that of sheriff, extends to the entire county. He is entitled to serve civil process in those counties contiguous to his own, and with a warrant, to make arrests beyond the limits of his county. To take office after election, the Texas constable must execute a bond with sureties and both take and sign a constitutional oath of office. Like all peace officers in Texas, constables can be held liable for a number of omissions or violations of duty.[3]

Civil court actions in the state of Texas begin with the service of different types of citations, writs, or subpoenas. The county or state charges various fees for such documents, and for legal service thereof to a defendant or witness in a civil suit. Deputy sheriffs, municipal police officers, constables, and private process servers are authorized to serve these civil papers. Service by a constable stands to offer a greater benefit to the local community by (a) bringing service fees into the treasury of the county where the service is made, (b) effecting quicker service because the constable is most familiar with the area and its citizens, and (c) minimizing any liability of service, because of the expertise of the constable in these matters.

THE CHANGING ROLE OF CONSTABLES

The town constable of the Old West metamorphosed long ago into the town or city marshal, and then the chief of police. In the many states, however, the county constable survives and thrives as an elected official at the precinct level. In others, the office has been abolished by either constitutional amendment or statute. Even in Texas, where the constable has survived numerous flags and constitutions, legislators have from time to time placed on the ballot various constitutional amendments for one or another county to abolish the office.

Often it is the smaller or more sparsely populated counties in Texas that have eliminated some county and precinct officials. Some counties now elect only a single constable for the entire county. In other counties, the office of constable is still on the books, but few, if any candidates run for the office, most likely because of the lack of experienced candidates, adequate funding, or local respect for the office. Nonetheless, in the majority of Texas counties, there is still an elected constable in each precinct.

Each elected constable can write his or her own internal guidelines, although all must comply with the code of criminal procedure. The result is that constables serving in different counties or in different precincts in the same county can undertake different duties and activities, reflecting the differences in the varying experience or attitudes of the constables themselves; or the attitudes, policies, and biases within county governments or other local law-enforcement agencies. Because they are usually dependent on county government for funding, and on other, mostly larger and more powerful, law-enforcement agencies for cooperation and services, Texas constables seldom reach their maximal potential, except in metropolitan precincts whose populations and budgets ensure they are both exceedingly busy and visible.

LICENSING AND TRAINING

Beginning in 1985, Texas constables were required to be licensed by the state of Texas as peace officers within two years after taking office.[4] To be licensed, a peace officer must take and pass the 560-hour Basic Peace Officers Course at a state-licensed law enforcement academy. A recognized law-enforcement agency must then employ and notify TCLEOSE that it is commissioning an individual as a peace officer. (Because each constable's office is a recognized law enforcement agency, it is often the constable who notifies TCLEOSE of the election of a constable or the appointment of a deputy constable.) To maintain his license, a peace officer must attend in-service training, a total of forty hours—some specified by TCLEOSE—in any twenty-four-month period. The training, education, and licensing of peace officers in the state of Texas have come a long way since the early 1970s.

Appendix C
Constables and Deputies Killed in the Line of Duty

An analysis of the records from the National Law Enforcement Memorial, although far from complete (particularly for the nineteenth century) confirms that at least 130 constables and deputy constables have died in the line of duty in twenty-nine states. The first U.S. constable confirmed killed in the line of duty was in 1825, in Venango County, Pennsylvania. Texas has lost the most, with twenty-five identified constables and deputy constables having been killed on duty in the twentieth century. Missouri is next, and California not far behind.

Of those ninety-two constables and deputy constables killed in the line of duty in the United States during the twentieth century, approximately forty-five percent died between 1920 and 1940, with twenty-seven of those deaths, averaging almost three per year, recorded during the 1920s. Even though murder and violence in the United States increased significantly, the six decades since 1940 claimed only another forty-five percent of the total number of constables killed in the line of duty across the United States in the twentieth century.

These national statistics are not, however, mirrored in Texas. During the twentieth century, almost thirty-three percent of Texas constables and deputy constables killed in the line of duty died between 1970 and 1979. Roughly another twenty-seven percent died in the 1980s and 1990s.

The following list identifies twenty-five constables and deputy constables killed in Texas in the twentieth century. I know of no list of constables killed in the line of duty in Texas during the nineteenth century, although this book begins that process by identifying John Selman, M. M. Givins, and others.

Date	County	Name	How Killed
9/29/98	Harris	Deputy Ray "Michael" Eakin	Shot during traffic stop
1/17/97	Jasper	Deputy Roy V. Richardson	Killed in auto accident
1/23/91	Nacogdoches	Constable Darrell Lunsford	Shot during traffic stop
5/20/85	Travis	Deputy David E. Nelson	Killed in auto accident
4/1/84	Polk	Constable Bill Garsee	Shot by unknown assassin
2/7/81	Nueces	Deputy Patrick S. Runyon	Shot during investigation
2/17/79	Hidalgo	Deputy Ricky S. Lewis	Shot by unknown person
9/25/78	Dallas	Deputy Joe M. Cox	Died of heart attack after chase and arrest
1/20/77	Zapata	Constable Manuel Gonzalez	Shot by assassin
6/7/75	Tarrant	Constable Earl F. Andrews	Shot during traffic stop
9/18/73	Pecos	Constable Allen Graham	Hit by vehicle while working at road block
6/29/72	Camp	Constable Daniel B. Tubbs	Shot by mentally disturbed man
3/25/71	Hill	Constable Milton Boortz	Shot during traffic stop
1/31/71	Orange	Constable Lewis O. Ford	Killed during arrest attempt
6/13/65	Atascosa	Constable George T. Hindes	Shot during traffic stop
10/10/62	Ellis	Constable James B. Wicker	Shot during arrest attempt
8/4/61	Duval	Constable Pedro R. Sendejo	Shot by burglar during arrest
2/16/34	Williamson	Constable Sam M. Moore	Shot taking prisoner to jail
11/18/29	Young	Constable Edward Lankford	Shot during investigation
12/23/25	Tarrant	Constable Robert F. Poe	Shot during investigation
3/24/25	Taylor	Constable George Reeves	Shot while attempting arrest
9/4/24	Dallas	Constable E. J. Harris	Shot by person/persons unknown
8/9/18	Freestone	Constable Bragg Dunbar	Shot by escaping burglars
3/25/17	Nueces	Constable Patrick W. Feely	Shot during investigation
7/22/10	Bell	Constable James W. Mitchell	Shot during investigation

NOTES

CHAPTER I. THE SPIT-DOG OF THE TREADMILL OF GOVERNMENT

1. *The Oxford Dictionary and Thesaurus*, American edition, New York: Oxford University Press, 1996.
2. Morris, *The Medieval Sheriff*, 46–49.
3. Livingston, *The Magna Carta*; Morris, *The Medieval Sheriff*, 159–229.
4. Ibid., 228–37.
5. Jones, *History of the Office of Constable*, 6–7.
6. Karraker, *The Seventeenth-Century Sheriff*, 56–57.
7. Ibid., 85–86.
8. Accomac[k] County Records, Virginia, 1640 to 1645, 82, Accomac[k], Virginia; Karraker, *The Seventeenth-Century Sheriff*, 197. In reproducing this oath, I have used modern English spelling and wording, which destroys none of its effect, but I hope makes the oath easier to understand.
9. Ibid., 86–87.
10. Ibid., 130–31.
11. Goebel and Naughton, *Law Enforcement in Colonial New York*, 68–69, 106–7, 110–11, 388.
12. Ibid., 338.
13. Goebel and Naughton, *Law Enforcement in Colonial New York*, 401–2, includes citation of various colonial laws of New York, amendments 7, 43, 29, 46, 617, 1665 to 1675.

CHAPTER II. TEXAS BEFORE INDEPENDENCE, 1820 TO 1836

The information contained herein on the period of pre-independence in Texas (1820–1836) comes from a number of sources. Primary among them are the assorted works of Eugene C. Barker, including the *Austin Papers* and *The Life of Stephen F. Austin*, along with various contributions to Texas State Historical Association publications such as the *Southwestern Historical Quarterly*. It should be noted that page numbers differ greatly between the various editions of Eugene C. Barker's *The Life of Stephen F. Austin*. The page numbers I quote are those from a first edition presentation volume in my possession, and not the other volumes of this excellent book.

1. Fehrenbach, *Lone Star*, 134–36; Haley, *Texas from Frontier to Spindletop*, 11–12. Moses Austin's son, Stephen F. Austin, was in New Orleans during his visit to Texas.
2. Eugene C. Barker, *The Life of Stephen F. Austin*, 35.
3. Ibid., 38. Stephen F. Austin was less than impressed with the dismal Spanish towns in Texas outside of San Antonio. It is said that he warmed to the idea of colonization only upon his visit to the Brazos and Colorado River areas.
4. Ibid., 39. The colonists' transformation of the alcalde into a justice of the peace as the first appointment in the colony is an example of the colonists' easy interaction with local or precinct officials similar to those from where they came.
5. Barker, *The Austin Papers*, 560, 583; *The Life of Stephen F. Austin*, 98–99; "The Government of Austin's Colony," 227–28. Alcalde Tumlinson wrote to

Baron de Bastrop in March 1823 regarding his previous appointment of a constable as the first law enforcement officer in the Colorado District. In January 1824, constables in the Colorado and Brazos Districts were bonded a year after their appointment and their beginning of service to the colony, in accordance with new civil and criminal codes approved by the Mexican Government. This practice has not changed in more than 175 years.

Some have mistakenly named the Texas Rangers as the first law enforcement group organized in Texas. Although Stephen F. Austin did mention the raising of a group of "rangers" in correspondence during August 1823, at least one and possibly two constables had already been appointed months earlier. Furthermore, there is every indication that the rangers Austin mentioned were to be a part of his militia and not peace officers in the colony.

6. Barker, *The Austin Papers* and "The Government of Austin's Colony," 226.

7. Joseph Kuykendahl, "Recollections of Captain Gibson Kuykendahl," *Texas State Historical Association Quarterly* 6(1904):39–40.

8. Texas State Historical Association, *The New Texas Handbook*, Vol. 1, 119–20; Barker, "The Government of Austin's Colony" and *The Austin Papers*, 729–32, 1131. The references further explain the appointment of the first law enforcement officers in Austin's colony.

9. Kuykendahl, "Recollections of Captain Gibson Kuykendahl," 49.

10. Texas State Historical Association, *The New Texas Handbook*, Vol. 1, 291–92; Barker, *The Austin Papers*, 729–32. *The New Texas Handbook* is invaluable in including both of the first two and several other constables appointed in Austin's colony.

11. John Bradford, *The General Instructor: or the Office, Duties, and Authority of Justices of the Peace, Sheriffs, Coroners, and Constables in the State of Kentucky, 1800*, Center for American History, University of Texas, Austin.

12. Barker, *The Austin Papers*, 755, 760, 792, 800–802, 1130. These references contain a number of letters that outline the activities, requirements, and documents handled by constables.

13. Texas State Historical Association, *The New Texas Handbook*, Vol. 1, 119.

14. Barker, *The Austin Papers*, 1064–122.

15. Barker, "The Government of Austin's Colony," 242–47.

16. Barker, *The Life of Stephen F. Austin*, 210–65.

17. Ball, *Desert Lawmen*, 5–6; Texas State Historical Association, *The New Texas Handbook*, Vol. 5, 516, 1058.

18. Barker, *The Life of Stephen F. Austin*, 210–12, and "The Government of Austin's Colony," 246–47.

19. Barker, "Minutes of the Ayuntamiento," 78–95.

20. Fehrenbach, *Lone Star*, 169–70; Haley, *Texas from Frontier to Spindletop*, 26; Barker, *The Life of Stephen F. Austin*, 296–328.

21. Fehrenbach, *Lone Star*, 170–72; Texas State Historical Association, *The New Texas Handbook*, Vol., 1, 291–92; Barker, *The Life of Stephen F. Austin*, 387–88; Rowe, "Disturbances at Anahuac in 1832."

22. Haley, *Texas from Frontier to Spindletop*, 28; Barker, *The Life of Stephen F. Austin*, 399–403.

23. Ibid., 404–29, and Barker, *The Austin Papers*.

24. Haley, *Texas from Frontier to Spindletop*, 29; Barker, *The Life of Stephen F. Austin*, 434–37.

25. Texas State Historical Association, *The New Texas Handbook*, Vol. 1, 291–92.

26. Ibid., 435–36.

27. Stovall, *Breaks of the Balcones*, 76–80; Texas State Historical Association, *The New Texas Handbook*, Vol. 4, 331; and Rister, "The Rio Grande Colony."

28. Weems and Weems, *Dreams of Empire*, 29.

29. Vol. 1 of Gammel, *The Laws of Texas*, outlines the proceedings and journals of the general council and provisional government of Texas, including, in Sec. 14 and 15, 1043, an ordinance and decree signed on January 22, 1836, by acting governor James Robinson, establishing a constable's appointment "in each and every municipality (future county) in Texas."

30. Ibid., 1043.

31. Fehrenbach, *Lone Star*, 191–98; Hardin, *Texas Iliad*, 88–91.

32. Ibid., 199–217; Fehrenbach, *Lone Star*, 219–34.

CHAPTER III. THE REPUBLIC OF TEXAS, 1836 TO 1845

1. Wallace, Vigness, and Ward, *Documents of Texas History*, 102. This is an excellent compilation, and an important addition to the bookshelf of any Texas history buff.

2. Fehrenbach, *Lone Star*, 214, 240–41.

3. Ibid., 247.

4. Ibid., 246.

5. Wallace, Vigness, and Ward, *Documents of Texas History*, 44–46. This excellent book contains copies of many important documents, summaries of important events, and biographical notes.

6. Hogan, *Texas Republic*, 245–46; Fehrenbach, *Lone Star*, 259.

7. Lack, *Texas Revolutionary Experience*, 61; Everton, *Handy Book for Genealogists*, 162–69; Texas State Archives Division, *Compiled Index to Elected & Appointed Officials of the Republic of Texas: 1835-1846*, v–xiii; Texas State Library, Austin, 1981; Gournay, *Texas Boundaries*, 29–32.

8. Texas State Archives, *Compiled Index*, v–xiii; Everton, *Handy Book for Genealogists*, 162–69; Gournay, *Texas Boundaries*, 30–34.

9. Fehrenbach, *Lone Star*, 249–50.

10. Texas State Archives, *Compiled Index* and 1838–1854 Elected/Appointed Officials, Reel No. 3498, Austin.

11. Texas State Historical Association, *The New Texas Handbook*, 369–70.

12. Texas State Archives, *Compiled Index*, vii.

13. Texas State Archives, 1838–1854 Elected/Appointed Officials, Reel No. 3498 and *Compiled Index*.

14. Texas State Archives, *Compiled Index*.

15. Texas State Historical Association, *The New Texas Handbook*, Vol. 4, 745.

16. Hogan, *Texas Republic*, 261–62.

17. Ibid., 262–66.

18. Weems and Weems, *Dreams of Empire*, 103.

19. Fehrenbach, *Lone Star*, 257–59; Weems and Weems, *Dreams of Empire*, 133–45.

20. Ibid., 145–56; Fehrenbach, *Lone Star*, 259.

21. Weems and Weems, *Dreams of Empire*, 139–45; Fehrenbach, *Lone Star*, 257–58.

22. McLeod, Report of the Council House Fight, written by the Inspector General to Governor Lamar, March 20, 1840, Center for American History, University of Texas, Austin; Weems and Weems, *Dreams of Empire*, 159–68; Brice, *Great Comanche Raid*, 20–28.

23. Ibid., 28–29; Weems and Weems, *Dreams of Empire*, 170.

24. Weems and Weems, *Dreams of Empire*, 170–72; Brice, *Great Comanche Raid*, 32–33.

25. Ibid., 38–42; Weems and Weems, *Dreams of Empire*, 173–76.

26. Brice, *Great Comanche Raid*, 62.

27. Greer, *Texas Ranger*, 64–66; Weems and Weems, *Dreams of Empire*, 206–8, 213–16.

28. Hogan, *Texas Republic*, 258; Fehrenbach, *Lone Star*, 261; Weems and Weems, *Dreams of Empire*, 222; Greer, *Texas Ranger*, 69–78.

29. Weems and Weems, *Dreams of Empire*, 285–86, 323.

30. Wallace, Vigness, and Ward, *Documents of Texas History*, 153; Weems and Weems, *Dreams of Empire*, 323; Fehrenbach, *Lone Star*, 265–67.

31. Weems and Weems, *Dreams of Empire*, 302–5, 324; Fehrenbach, *Lone Star*, 265–67.

CHAPTER IV. THE LONE STAR STATE, 1846 TO 1873

1. Greer, *Texas Ranger*, 64–78; Williams, *Sam Houston*, 213–18, 229–250.

2. Haley, *Texas from Frontier to Spindletop*, 129–31.

3. Gammel, *The Laws of Texas*, 261–65.

4. Haley, *Texas from Frontier to Spindletop*, 134–35.

5. Ibid., 137.

6. Ibid., 131.

7. Texas State Historical Association, *The New Texas Handbook*, Vol. 5, 966–67.

8. Williams, *Sam Houston*, 336–48.

9. Texas State Archives, 1862, 1864 Elected Officials, Reel No. 3499, 3500.

10. Ibid.; Webb, *The Texas Rangers*, 41.

11. Richter, *The Army in Texas during Reconstruction*, 129–36.

12. Martin, *Texas Divided*, 129–36; Richter, *The Army in Texas during Reconstruction*, 161–66; Haley, *Texas from Frontier to Spindletop*, 180–81.

13. Texas State Archives, 1866 Elected Officials, Reel 3501.

14. Haley, *Texas from Frontier to Spindletop*, 180; Texas State Historical Association, *The New Texas Handbook*, Vol. 2, 282.

15. Texas State Archives, 1866, 1870, 1872 Elected Officials, Reels 3501, 3502.

16. Richter, 133–36; Nunn, *Texas Under Carpetbaggers*, 177–209.

17. Wallace, Vigness, and Ward, *Documents of Texas History*, 214.

18. Ibid., 214.

19. Texas State Archives, 1872 Elected Officials, Reel 3502.

20. Martin, *Texas Divided*, 140–41; Nunn, *Texas Under Carpetbaggers*, 18–19.

21. Ibid., 29–31, 38.

22. Ibid., 43–65; Haley, *Texas from Frontier to Spindletop*, 187.

23. Nunn, *Texas Under Carpetbaggers*, 62–63.

24. Ibid., 63–64.

25. Ibid., 67–68.

26. Ibid., 70–75.

27. Ibid., 81–86.
28. Ibid., 64–65.
29. Dykstra, *The Cattle Towns*, 101.
30. Ibid., 123–25, 128–48.
31. Nunn, *Texas Under Carpetbaggers*, 177–92.
32. *Report of the Adjutant General of Texas for 1872*, Texas State Archives and Library, Austin.

CHAPTER V. THE FAR WEST, 1874 TO 1900

1. Texas Almanac, *Dallas Morning News* (1995):379–446.
2. Webb, *The Story of the Texas Rangers*, 1–2, 41–46.
3. Gammel, *The Laws of Texas*, Vol. 7, 1389.
4. Sonnichsen, *Pass of the North*, 144, 151, 160.
5. Ibid., 168–69, 173.
6. Metz, *Dallas Stoudenmire*, 70–72; Sonnichsen, *Pass of the North*, 213.
7. Metz, *Dallas Stoudenmire*, 3.
8. Egloff, *El Paso Lawman*, 55–58; Metz, *Dallas Stoudenmire*, 3–9.
9. Ibid., 39-40.
10. Ibid.; Texas State Archives, 1880 Elected Officials, Reel 3505, Austin. Although Gus Krempkau's name does not appear among the elected officials of 1880 (Reel 3505) in the Texas State Archives, it is well documented that Krempkau was a constable at the time. We must assume, therefore, either that he was hired as a "town" constable in El Paso, or (because of his described activities outside the town limits) he was appointed and not elected to the then vacant job of constable of Precinct No. 1, El Paso County in late 1880 or early 1881.
11. Metz, *Dallas Stoudenmire*, 39.
12. Ibid., 39–40.
13. Egloff, *El Paso Lawman*, 88; Metz, *Dallas Stoudenmire*, 40–41.
14. Ibid., 42–43.
15. O'Neal, *Encyclopedia of Western Gunfighters*, 303–4.
16. Holden, "Law & Lawlessness," 201–2.
17. O'Neal, *Encyclopedia of Western Gunfighters*, 260–61. Jim Reed, who had been married to Belle Starr, had a long history of law-breaking, including arson at the Scott County, Arkansas Courthouse, for which he served a year in the Arkansas State Penitentiary, and horse stealing. He was killed near Paris, Texas, in 1874.
18. Miller, *Bounty Hunter*, 155–61.
19. Metz, *John Selman, Gunfighter*, 136–37; Texas State Archives, 1892 Elected Officials, Reel 3510; DeArment, *George Scarborough*, 68–69; Sonnichsen, *Pass of the North*, 317.

John Selman was like hundreds of *pistoleros*, or would-be gunfighters in the Old West. Those already good with a gun or wannabes sometimes drifted from a life of crime in one community, to wearing a badge and enforcing the law in the next place they landed, and sometimes back to being chased by the law. There are many, many examples of Texas Rangers, constables, sheriffs and their deputies, and town marshals all playing this same role. Some of those who have written about John Selman obviously have little if any liking for the man—not that a liking for a historical character is needed to write candidly. But John Selman seems often to have come out on the losing side when writers speculate on the unclear events of his life. My purpose in this book is not to make Selman a saint, but to give him the same benefit of the doubt as that given to dozens of former sheriffs and Texas Rangers who sometimes "went bad." John Selman seems to have been one of the hardest working law-enforcement officers in El Paso in the early 1890s. There were many other lawmen, mostly deputy U.S. marshals, and present or former Texas Rangers, who hung around this oasis in Far West Texas, but the court records of El Paso are full of arrests made and citations executed by John Selman.

20. Metz, *John Selman, Gunfighter*, 129, 133–34; *Dallas Stoudenmire*, 114–19.

21. Metz, *John Selman, Gunfighter*, 129–36.

22. Ibid., 64–89.

23. Ibid., 91–126.

24. Ibid., 16, 203.

25. Sonnichsen, *Pass of the North*, 137; Metz, *John Selman, Gunfighter*, 138, 145–46, 153.

26. Ibid., 153, 157.

27. Ibid., 146–47.

28. Collinson, *Life in the Saddle*, 98–99; Metz, *John Selman, Gunfighter*, 148.

29. DeArment, *George Scarborough*, 72–73. DeArment, in his excellent book on George Scarborough, writes that "Texas Ranger Joe McKidrict and Constable Leon Chavez had jumped the back fence into the yard" and arrived together at Tillie Howard's Sporting House after the whistle was blown. I suggest that Chavez may have been a deputy constable visiting from another jurisdiction, or appointed constable by the town of El Paso. He apparently was not an El Paso County constable, as he does not appear in the list of elected officials. Collinson mentions a "deputy" arriving with McKidrict.

30. Ibid., 73; Metz, *John Selman, Gunfighter*, 149.

31. Ibid.,149–50.

32. Ibid., 150.

33. Texas State Archives, 1894 Elected Officials, Reel 3511.

34. Ibid.

35. Metz, *John Selman, Gunfighter*, 160; Metz, *John Wesley Hardin*, 208.

36. Ibid., 12–13, 33, 40–43, 72–77, 137–39, 168–71.

37. Ibid., 229–35.

38. DeArment, *George Scarborough*, 77–99, 116–17; Metz, *John Wesley Hardin*, 222, 246–47.

39. Ibid., 247–49.

40. DeArment, *George Scarborough*, 104–5; Metz, *John Wesley Hardin*, 249.

41. Ibid., 249–52; DeArment, *George Scarborough*, 109. John Selman is occasionally mentioned as taking part in the killing of Martin Morose. This just will not work, because no one directly associated with the case has ever seriously accused Selman of participating in the Morose murder.

42. Dixson, *Richland Crossing*, 358; Metz, *John Wesley Hardin*, 256–57.

43. Ibid., 236–42, 260–64; Metz, *John Selman, Gunfighter*, 170–171.

44. DeArment, *George Scarborough*, 128; Dixson, *Richland Crossing*, 360; Metz, *John Wesley Hardin*, 264–65; *El Paso Daily Times*, August 20, 1895.

45. Metz, *John Wesley Hardin*, 265.

46. Dixson, *Richland Crossing*, 360; DeArment, *George Scarborough*, 131.

47. Ibid., 268, 277–78; Metz, *John Selman, Gunfighter*, 182–93.

48. Ibid., 191, 195; O'Neal, *Encyclopedia of Western Gunfighters*, 65.

49. Metz, *John Wesley Hardin*, 278.
50. Ibid., 279; O'Neal, *Encyclopedia of Western Gunfighters*, 274.
51. Metz, *John Wesley Hardin*, 266–68; Metz, *John Selman, Gunfighter*, 175–81.
52. O'Neal, *Encyclopedia of Western Gunfighters*, 276–79; Metz, *John Selman, Gunfighter*, 63, 204–5.
53. Ibid., 178–81; Metz, *John Wesley Hardin*, 247–52.
54. Ibid., 268–71; Metz, *John Selman, Gunfighter*, 191, 195; Dixson, *Richland Crossing*, 360; DeArment, *George Scarborough*, 127–28.
55. Ibid., 128; Metz, *John Wesley Hardin*, 264–65, 268–71, 279.
56. Ibid., 272–77; Metz, *John Selman, Gunfighter*, 183–93.
57. Miller, *Bounty Hunter*, 210–12.
58. *Dallas Morning News* (July 20, 1997):35A, 36A.
59. Fisher and Dykes, *King Fisher*, 8–9.
60. Combs, *Gunsmoke in the Redlands*, 29–37.

CHAPTER VI. THE TEXAS PANHANDLE, 1874 TO 1900

1. Robertson and Robertson, *Panhandle Pilgrimage*, 87–101.
2. Ibid., 98–101.
3. Ibid., 103–26.
4. Ibid., 100, 196–197.
5. Ibid., 197.
6. McCarty, *Maverick Town*, 53–56 ; Robertson and Robertson, *Panhandle Pilgrimage*, 129–42.
7. Ibid., 143–53.
8. Gournay, *Texas Boundaries*, 95–107; Robertson and Robertson, *Panhandle Pilgrimage*, 180, 199.
9. Texas State Archives, 1878 Elected Officials, Reel 3504; Robertson and Robertson, *Panhandle Pilgrimage*, 199.
10. Texas State Archives, 1878 Elected Officials, Reel 3504; Robertson and Robertson, *Panhandle Pilgrimage*, 198–99; Gournay, *Texas Boundaries*, 106–7.
11. O'Neal, *Henry Brown*, 74–76; McCarty, *Maverick Town*, 81; Robertson and Robertson, *Panhandle Pilgrimage*, 214–15.
12. Ibid., 168–71.
13. Metz, *Pat Garrett*, 71–72.
14. Robertson and Robertson, *Panhandle Pilgrimage*, 171; Metz, *Pat Garrett*, 71–72.
15. Texas State Archives, 1878 Elected Officials, Reel 3504; Metz, *Pat Garrett*, 96–97.
16. Ibid., 97–117.
17. Robertson and Robertson, *Panhandle Pilgrimage*, 181, 182, 187–89.
18. Ibid., 207–10.
19. Texas State Archives, 1880 and 1881 Elected Officials, Reel 3505; McCarty, *Maverick Town*; Robertson and Robertson, *Panhandle Pilgrimage*, 210.
20. Ibid., 211, 212, 217.
21. O'Neal, *Henry Brown*, 78; McCarty, *Maverick Town*, 96–97.
22. Ibid., 97–98; O'Neal, *Henry Brown*, 79–80.
23. McCarty, *Maverick Town*, 98–99; O'Neal, *Henry Brown*, 80–81.
24. McCarty, *Maverick Town*, 99–101; O'Neal, *Henry Brown*, 81–82.

25. Texas State Archives, 1882 Election Results, Reel 3506; Robertson and Robertson, *Panhandle Pilgrimage*, 200–203.

26. Ibid., 218–19.

27. Texas State Archives, 1882 Elected Officials, Reel 3506.

28. Gober, *Cowboy Justice*, 86–89, 100–106; Robertson and Robertson, *Panhandle Pilgrimage*, 282.

29. Gober, *Cowboy Justice*, 106; Robertson and Robertson, *Panhandle Pilgrimage*, 283.

30. Crudgington, "Old Town Amarillo," Robertson and Robertson, *Panhandle Pilgrimage*, 282–83.

31. Texas State Archives, 1887 Elected Officials, Reel 3508; Gober, *Cowboy Justice*, 108; Key, *In the Cattle Country*, 42, 300; Crudgington, "Old Town Amarillo."

32. Key, *In the Cattle Country*, 43; Robertson and Robertson, *Panhandle Pilgrimage*, 283–86.

33. Texas State Archives, 1888 Elected Officials, Reel 3509; Key, *In the Cattle Country*, 300.

34. File Box 15, Case 1, County Clerks Office, Amarillo, Potter County; Gober, *Cowboy Justice*, 298, note 3; Key, *In the Cattle Country*, 59. An unusually complete file is maintained on the grand jury and trial of Gober in the Potter County Clerk's Office. Many of the documents referenced hereafter can be viewed in this file. I am grateful to Constable David S. Crawford in Amarillo for first advising me of this file.

35. Key, *In the Cattle Country*, 59–60.

36. Ibid., 60.

37. Ibid.; Gober, *Cowboy Justice*, 125, 298, note 3. Jim Gober, on page 125, writes that he saw Constable Givins attempting to shake down several "gamblers" in the back room of the Collins saloon; then Givins turned toward him and drew his gun. Gober says he then shot Givins. If Gober believed this scenario when he shot Givins, we must question his judgment. We know from several eyewitnesses that Constable Givins was actually serving court-ordered arrest warrants on several people for illegal gambling when Gober arrived, and was not shaking them down, as Sheriff Gober claims. According to witnesses, Gober was in the room long enough to understand Givins was on duty. Furthermore, Givins drew his gun in response to a threat made on him by a bystander. Gober's story is completely different from the depositions given by almost a dozen witnesses. According to several eyewitnesses, including J. A. Williams, Gober also stated immediately after the shooting that the shot was accidental. This is contrary to his claim (p. 125) that he shot Givins because Givins drew his gun.

38. Spikes, *A History of Crosby County*, 215; Key, *In the Cattle Country*, 60.

39. Ibid.

40. January 12, 1889, Voluntary Statement of M. M. Givins, File Box 15, Case 1, County Clerk Office, Amarillo, Potter County.

41. Key, *In the Cattle Country*, 60.

42. Gober, *Cowboy Justice*, 125, 298, note 3; January 12, 1889, Voluntary Statement of M. M. Givins, File Box 15, Case 1, County Clerk's Office, Amarillo, Potter County.

43. Key, *In the Cattle Country*, 60; Gober, *Cowboy Justice*, 140, 298, note 3. There is a serious lack of credibility in Gober's claims that, firstly, Constable Givins was "appointed" and unknown to him, and secondly, that Jacob Lowmiller, who was

appointed to replace Givins, was unknown to him, when both men had been on the same ballot as Gober just a few months before. Lowmiller had even run for the same office of sheriff as Gober.

44. Key, *In the Cattle Country*, 61.
45. Crudgington, "Old Town Amarillo"; Key, *In the Cattle Country*, 61.
46. Crudgington, "Old Town Amarillo"; Key, *In the Cattle Country*, 61.
47. Ibid., 61–62, 300–301; Gober, *Cowboy Justice*, 145–51. Gober claims to have been elected sheriff again in 1890. This is not true. In fact he was removed as sheriff in late 1889, and A. F. Criswell was appointed to take his place. M. Worden was then elected sheriff in Potter County in 1890.
48. Robertson and Robertson, *Panhandle Pilgrimage*, 295, 308.

Chapter VII. Reform and Hard Work, 1900 to 1946

1. Richardson, Anderson, and Wallace, *Texas, the Lone Star State*, 289–306; Calvert and deLeon, *The History of Texas*, 227–31, 270–85; Fehrenbach, *Lone Star*, 629–36.
2. Webb, *The Story of the Texas Rangers*, 5, 133.
3. Rigler and Rigler, *In the Line of Duty*, 25; Webb, *The Story of the Texas Rangers*, 133–34.
4. Smith, *Units of Local Government*, 18–22; Texas State Historical Association, *The New Texas Handbook*, Vol. 2, 369–70.
5. Sitton, *Texas High Sheriffs*, 3.
6. Smith, *Units of Local Government*, 18–22; Texas State Historical Association, *The New Texas Handbook*, Vol. 2, 369–70.
7. Laake, *History of Paige and Vicinity*, 43, 167.
8. Texas State Historical Association, *The New Texas Handbook*, Vol. 3, 586.
9. Ibid., 589; Cox, *Silver Stars and Sixguns*, 16.
10. Texas State Historical Association, *The New Texas Handbook*, Vol. 3, 586.
11. Wilbanks, *Forgotten Heroes Bell Co.*, 7–8.
12. Ibid.
13. Ibid., 8.
14. Ibid.
15. Ibid., 9.
16. *Temple Daily Telegram*, July 23–26, 1910.
17. Wilbanks, *Forgotten Heroes Bell Co.*, 10–11; *Temple Daily Telegram*, July 22, 1910.
18. Wilbanks, *Forgotten Heroes Bell Co.*, 12–13, 16.
19. Ibid., 15–19.
20. *Corpus Christi Caller and Daily Herald*, March 25, 1917.
21. Ibid., April 12, 1917.
22. Ibid., March 28–April 9, 1917.
23. Freestone County Commission, *History Freestone Co.*, 59.
24. Ibid.
25. Ibid.
26. Ibid.
27. Ibid.
28. Robertson and Robertson, *Panhandle Pilgrimage*, 319–23.
29. Ibid., 326–30.

30. *Dallas Morning News,* September 5, 1924; Interview with Fred Harris, January 1998.

31. *Dallas Morning News,* September 7, 1924.

32. Interview with Fred Harris, January 1998.

33. Fuller, *Gunfire on Front Street,* 12. The author wishes to thank Abilene police officer David Fuller for his generosity in providing information on the murder of Constable George L. Reeves of Taylor County.

34. Fuller, *Gunfire on Front Street,* 12.

35. Ibid., 12–13.

36. *Dallas Morning News,* December 24, 1925.

37. Ibid.

38. Ibid., November 19, 1929.

39. Sitton, *Texas High Sheriffs,* 29.

40. Ibid., 30–31.

41. Texas State Historical Association, *The New Texas Handbook,* Vol. 6, 172; Sitton, *Texas High Sheriffs,* 277.

42. *Williamson County Sun,* February 23, 1934.

43. Ibid.; Personal communication with Dan Martinets of Williamson County, who as a child witnessed the shootings.

44. *Williamson County Sun,* February 23, 1934.

45. Ibid.

46. Ibid.

47. Ibid., March 16–April 27, 1934.

48. Sitton, *Texas High Sheriffs,* 99, 278.

49. Ibid., 99.

50. Ibid., 97–98.

51. Day, *Captain Clint Peoples,* 18–19.

52. Ibid., 18.

53. Ibid., 19–29.

54. Ibid., 34.

55. Ibid., 19–35.

CHAPTER VIII. MODERN TEXAS, 1946 TO 1999

1. *Alice Daily Echo,* August 6, 1961.

2. Ibid.

3. Ibid., August 30, 1961.

4. *Dallas Morning News,* October 11, 1962.

5. Ibid.

6. *Pleasanton Express,* June 16, 1965.

7. Ibid.

8. Ibid.

9. Ibid., June 30, 1965.

10. Ibid., June 30–July 7, 1965.

11. Ibid., July 7, 1965.

12. Analysis of National Law Enforcement Memorial data.

13. *Beaumont Enterprise,* February 2, 1971.

14. *Port Arthur News,* February 2–5, 1971.

15. Ibid., February 5–9, 1971.

16. *Dallas Morning News,* March 22–27, 1971.
17. Ibid.
18. *Pittsburg Gazette,* July 6, 1972. I am indebted to Constable Jerry D. Farmer, Precinct No. 1 of Camp County, for providing information on the murder of Daniel B. Tubbs.
19. *Pittsburg Gazette,* July 6, 1972.
20. Ibid.
21. Ibid.
22. Department of Public Safety, *Crime in Texas, 1977,* 28.
23. *Dallas Morning News,* September 20, 1973; *Fort Worth Star-Telegram,* September 20, 1973.
24. Interview with Borta Andrews, widow of Earl Andrews, on April 3, 1997.
25. Ibid.; Department of Public Safety, *Crime in Texas, 1975,* 42–43.
26. Interview with Borta Andrews.
27. Department of Public Safety, *Crime in Texas, 1975,* 42–43.
28. Interview with Judge Hector Lopez in Zapata on October 29, 1997.
29. Ibid.; Department of Public Safety, *Crime in Texas, 1977,* 42–43.
30. Interview with Judge Hector Lopez.
31. Interview with Chief Deputy Constable Gary Edwards, Precinct No. 3, Dallas County, on January 5, 1998.
32. Ibid.
33. Ibid.
34. *The Monitor,* McAllen, Texas, February 18, 1979.
35. Ibid., February 18, 27, 1979.
36. *Corpus Christi Times,* February 14, 1981.
37. Ibid.
38. Ibid., March 6-August 8, 1981.
39. Ibid., August 6, 1981.
40. Ibid., February 23, 1982.
41. The story of Constable Bill Garsee was developed during interviews from October 1996 to March 1997 with Teenie Garsee, widow of Bill Garsee; his brother A. J. Garsee in Moscow, Texas; Polk County District Attorney Investigator C. R. Staton; Polk County Constable John Holt, Precinct No. 1; Anthony Page, president of the Citizens State Bank in Corrigan; John D. Clifton, owner of the Chevrolet dealership and a sometime employer of Garsee; Mike Nicholson, who sold gasoline to the alleged assassin in Corrigan; Texas Ranger Don Morrison; Jack Long, another rodeo clown and friend of Bill Garsee; numerous newspaper clippings provided by Garsee's family and friends from San Augustine, and Polk County newspapers from 1984 to 1987; court records, and various reports from several law enforcement agencies, along with personal observations of the author.
42. Interviews with Teenie Garsee, Anthony Page, and John Clifton in October 1996.
43. Interview with Teenie Garsee.
44. Ibid.
45. Interview with C. R. Staton, Investigator for Polk County District Attorney's office, in October 1996; interview with Texas Ranger Don Morrison in November 1996; *San Augustine Tribune.*
46. *Corrigan Times,* May 10, 1984; interview with C. R. Staton.
47. Ibid.

48. Interviews with Mike Nicholson, Corrigan, and C. R. Staton.
49. Ibid.
50. Interview with Ed Kirk, Austin, September, 1997.
51. Ibid.
52. The story of Constable Darrell Lunsford was developed through interviews from October 1996 to August 6, 1997 with Shirley Lunsford, his widow, in Houston; D. J. (Darrell) Lunsford, son of Darrell Lunsford in Garrison; former Precinct No. 3 Justice of the Peace Harold Bogue; Precinct No. 1 Constable Bill Ball; Deputy Constable T. M. Peterson; Precinct No. 2 Constable Eddie Upshaw; and District Attorney Tim James, all of Nacogdoches County; several videotapes of the murder of Darrell Lunsford; the *Reader's Digest* article, "The Cop Who Caught His Killers," by Mark Roman, November 1993, 67–72, and numerous newspaper articles.
53. Interview with Shirley Lunsford, widow of Darrell Lunsford, on August 6, 1997.
54. Interviews with Nacogdoches County Constable Bill Ball, Precinct No. 1, from October 1996 to June 1997; with Deputy Constable T. M. Peterson in October 1996; Mark Roman, "The Cop Who Caught His Killers," *Reader's Digest,* November, 1993, 67–72, and the videotape of Darrell Lunsford's murder.
55. Interviews with Shirley Lunsford, August 6, 1997, and Nacogdoches County District Attorney Tim James, between January and June 1997.
56. Interviews with Tim James and Constable Bill Ball of Precinct No. 1, between January and June 1997.
57. Interview with Harold Bogue.
58. Interview with D. J. (Darrell) Lunsford, son of Darrell Lunsford, in October 1996; videotape of Darrell Lunsford's murder; Roman, "The Cop Who Caught His Killers," 67–72.
59. Ibid.; interview with Shirley Lunsford.
60. Roman, "The Cop Who Caught His Killers," 67–72; videotape of Darrell Lunsford's murder.
61. Roman, "The Cop Who Caught His Killers"; videotape of Darrell Lunsford's murder.
62. Interviews with Tim James and Bill Ball; Roman, "The Cop Who Caught His Killers."
63. Ibid.
64. Ibid.
65. *Jasper Newsboy,* January 24, 1996; DPS Accident Report, dated January 30, 1996, of incident in the public record; personal communication with Jasper Sheriff Billy Rolls.
66. Interview with Chief Deputy Constable J. C. Mosier, Precinct No. 1, Harris County, on December 1, 1998; Internet report of the shooting of Deputy Eakin, dated September 29, 1998, and provided by Pam Nickel, Information Technician in the Crime Records Service, Texas Department of Public Safety.

Appendix A. Some Constables Outside of Texas

1. Rosa, *The West of Wild Bill Hickok,* 3–35; O'Neal, *Encyclopedia of Western Gunfighters,* 134.
2. Rosa, *They Called Him Wild Bill,* 22–27.

3. Ibid., 27–30.
4. O'Neal, *Encyclopedia of Western Gunfighters*, 135–36; Rosa, *They Called Him Wild Bill*, 87–139.
5. Miller and Snell, *Great Gunfighters of Kansas*, 437–39.
6. Ibid.
7. Dykstra, *Cattle Towns*, 138–39, 143.
8. Ibid., 138–39.
9. O'Neal, *Encyclopedia of Western Gunfighters*, 21–22.
10. Ibid.
11. Ibid., 109.
12. Miller and Snell, *Great Gunfighters of Kansas*, 95–97.
13. DeMattos, *Mysterious Gunfighter*, 32–44.
14. Ibid., 42–49.
15. Miller and Snell, *Great Gunfighters of Kansas*, 321–23.
16. DeMattos, *Mysterious Gunfighter*, 56–60.
17. Ibid., 151–79.
18. Chaput, *Virgil Earp*, 2–6.
19. Ibid., 8–9.
20. Boyer, *Wyatt Earp: The Facts*, Vol. 4, 4–8.
21. Ibid., 7–9.
22. Tefertiller, *Wyatt Earp*, 4–5; Boyer, *Wyatt Earp: The Facts*, 8–9; Chaput, *Virgil Earp*, 17–26; O'Neal, *Encyclopedia of Western Gunfighters*, 100–1.
23. Chaput, *Virgil Earp*, 32–33, 44.
24. Ibid., 47.
25. Tefertiller, *Wyatt Earp*, 56–57; O'Neal, *Encyclopedia of Western Gunfighters*, 247–48.
26. Ibid., 99.
27. Chaput, *Virgil Earp*, 166–79.
28. Wilbanks, *Forgotten Heroes, Greenville Co.*, 5–6.
29. National Law Enforcement Memorial data.
30. National Law Enforcement Memorial data.
31. Wilbanks, *Forgotten Heroes, Greenville Co.*, 80–81.
32. Ibid., 75–76.
33. Ibid., 76–79.
34. Wilbanks, *Forgotten Heroes, Dade Co.*, 54–55.
35. Ibid., 79.
36. Ibid., 76–77.
37. Ibid., 78–79.
38. Morris, *Legacy of Buford Pusser*, 22–23.
39. Ibid., 23–26.
40. Ibid., 28–32.
41. Ibid., 32–34.
42. Ibid., 49–54.
43. Ibid., 54–57.
44. Ibid., 61–109.
45. Wilbanks, *Forgotten Heroes, Greenville Co.*, 152.
46. Ibid., 152–53.
47. Ibid., 153–56.

Appendix B. A Look at Today's Constables

1. Texas Code of Criminal Procedures, Article 2.13; Texas Local Government Code, Article 86.024.

2. *Vernon's Revised Criminal Statutes,* Article 4413.

3. *Texas Peace Officers Manual.*

4. Government Code, Chapter 415, Section 415.015, and 415.05.

BIBLIOGRAPHY

BOOKS AND ARTICLES

Armstrong, Marion, "Memoirs." In John L. McCarty Collection, Amarillo Public Library, Amarillo.

Ball, Larry D. *Desert Lawmen: The High Sheriffs of New Mexico and Arizona 1846–1912.* Albuquerque: University of New Mexico Press, 1992.

Bandera County Historical Commission. *The Bandera County Historian,* various issues from 1980 to 1994.

Barker, Eugene C. "The Government of Austin's Colony 1821–1831." *The Southwestern Historical Quarterly* 21(1918):223–52.

———. *The Life of Stephen F. Austin, Founder of Texas, 1793–1836.* Nashville: Cokesbury Press, 1925.

———, editor. "Minutes of the Ayuntamiento of San Felipe de Austin 1828–1832," *Southwestern Historical Quarterly* 22(1)(July, 1918):78–95.

———, compiler and editor. *The Austin Papers,* Vols. 1 and 2. Washington, D.C.: Government Printing Office, 1924 and 1928. Vol. 3. Austin: University of Texas Press, 1927.

Bartholomew, Ed. *Wyatt Earp: The Man and the Myth.* Toyahvale: Frontier Book, 1964.

Benavides, Adan Jr., editor. *The Bexar Archives (1717–1836), A Name Guide.* Austin: University of Texas Press, 1989.

Boethel, Paul C. *History of Lavaca County.* Austin: Von-Boeckmann-Jones, 1959.

Boyer, Glenn G., *Wyatt Earp: Facts,* Vol. 6, *Wyatt Wears His First Badge, Lamar, Missouri, March 5, 1870.* Rodeo, N.M.: Historical Research Associates, 1997.

Bradford, John, *The General Instructor: or the Office, Duties and Authority of Justices of the Peace, Sheriffs, Coroners and Constables in the State of Kentucky, 1800.* Austin: Center for American History, University of Texas.

Brice, Donaly E. *The Great Comanche Raid.* Austin: Eakin Press, 1987.

Browning, James A. *Violence Was No Stranger: A Guide to the Grave Sites of Famous Westerners.* Stillwater: Barbed Wire Press, 1993.

———. *The Western Reader's Guide: A Selected Bibliography of Non-Fiction Magazines 1953–1991.* Stillwater: Barbed Wire Press, 1992.

Calvert, Robert A., and Arnoldo deLeon, *The History of Texas.* Wheeling: Harlan Davidson, 1997.

Cashion, Ty. *A Texas Frontier: The Clear Fork Country and Fort Griffin, 1859–1887.* Norman: University of Oklahoma Press, 1996.

Chaput, Donald. *Virgil Earp Western Peace Officer.* Norman: University of Oklahoma Press, 1994.

Collinson, Frank. *Life in the Saddle.* Norman: University of Oklahoma Press, 1963.

Combs, Joe F. *Gunsmoke in the Redlands.* San Antonio: Naylor, 1968.

Cordova, J. de. *Texas: Her Resources and Her Public Men.* Austin: Texian Press, 1969.

Cox, Mike. *Silver Stars and Sixguns: The Texas Rangers.* Austin: Texas Department of Public Safety, undated pamphlet.

———. *Texas Ranger Tales, Stories That Need Telling.* Plano: Republic of Texas Press, 1997.

Crudgington, John, "Old Town Amarillo," reprinted from *Panhandle Plains Historical Review.* Amarillo: Russell Stationery, 1957.

Cunningham, Eugene. *Triggernometry: A Gallery of Gunfighters.* Caxton, 1941. Reprinted, New York: Barnes & Noble, 1996.

Day, James M. *Captain Clint Peoples, Texas Ranger.* Waco: Texian Press, 1980.

DeArment, Robert K. *George Scarborough: The Life and Death of a Lawman on the Closing Frontier.* Norman: University of Oklahoma Press, 1992.

Debo, Darrell. *Burnet County History,* Vol. 1. Austin: Eakin Press, 1979.

DeMattos, Jack. *Mysterious Gunfighter: The Story of Dave Mather.* College Station: Creative Publishing, 1992.

DeShields, James T. *Border Wars of Texas;* revised edition. Austin: State House Press, 1993.

Dixson, Walter Clay. *Richland Crossing, A Portrait of Texas Pioneers.* Fort Worth: Peppermill Publishing, 1994.

Durham, George. *Taming the Nueces Strip.* Austin: University of Texas Press, 1962.

Dykstra, Robert R. *The Cattle Towns.* New York: Alfred A. Knopf, 1968.

Edwards, Harold L., "Lawmen's Fight for Just Rewards," *Wild West Magazine* (October 1997): 62–66.

Egloff, Fred E. *El Paso Lawman G. W. Campbell.* College Station: Creative Publications, 1982.

Everton, George, editor. *Fourth Edition of the Handy Book for Genealogists.* Everton Publications, 1981.

Fehrenbach, T. R. *Lone Star: A History of Texas and the Texans.* New York: Macmillan, 1968.

Fisher, O. C., and J. C. Dykes. *King Fisher His Life and Times.* Norman: University of Oklahoma Press, 1966.

Ford, John Salmon. *Rip Ford's Texas,* edited by Stephen B. Oates. Austin: University of Texas Press, 1963.

Freestone County Historical Commission. *History of Freestone County.* Winston-Salem: Hunter, 1978.

Fuller, David. *Gunfire on Front Street, A History of the Abilene Police Department 1881–1993.* Abilene: Chaco Publications, 1993.

Gammel, H.P.M., compiler and arranger. *The Laws of Texas, 1822–1905,* 12 vols. Austin: Gammel.

Gard, Wayne. *Frontier Justice.* Norman: University of Oklahoma Press, 1949.

Gillett, James B. *Fugitives from Justice, The Notebook of Texas Ranger Sergeant James B. Gillett.* Austin: State House Press, 1997.

———. *Six Years with the Texas Rangers.* Lincoln: University of Nebraska Press, 1921.

Gober, Jim. *Cowboy Justice: The Tale of a Texas Lawman,* edited by J. R. Gober and B. Byron Price. Lubbock: Texas Tech University Press, 1997.

Goebel, Julius Jr., and T. Raymond Naughton. *Law Enforcement in Colonial New York: A Study in Criminal Behavior, 1664–1776.* Montclair, N.J.: Patterson Smith, 1970.

Gournay, Luke. *Texas Boundaries, Evolution of the State's Counties.* College Station: Texas A & M University Press, 1995.

Gray, Frank S. *Pioneering in Southwest Texas.* Austin: privately published by Frank Gray, 1949.

Greer, James K. *Texas Ranger, Jack Hays in the Texas Frontier.* College Station: Texas A & M University Press, 1993.

Haley, James L. *Texas From the Frontier to Spindletop.* New York: St. Martin's Press, 1985.

Haley, J. Evetts. *Jeff Milton: A Good Man With a Gun.* Norman: University of Oklahoma Press, 1948.

Hardin, Stephen L. *Texas Iliad: A Military History of the Texas Revolution 1835–1836.* Austin: University of Texas Press, 1994.

Harkey, Dee. *The Life of a New Mexico Lawman: Mean as Hell.* Santa Fe: Ancient City Press, 1989.

Hogan, William R. *The Texas Republic: A Social and Economic History.* Norman: University of Oklahoma Press, 1946.

Holden, W. C. "Law and Lawlessness on the Texas Frontier 1875–1890." *Southwestern Historical Quarterly* 44(2)(October 1940):188–203.

Hunter, J. Marvin. *A Brief History of Bandera County.* Bandera: privately published by J. Marvin Hunter, 1949.

Jones, Billy M. *The Search for Maturity, 1875–1900.* Austin: Steck-Vaughn, 1965.

Jones, Dean. *History of the Office of Constable.* Texas Justice Court Publication, San Marcos, brochure, no date.

Karraker, Cyrus Harreld. *The Seventeenth-Century Sheriff: A Comparative Study of the Sheriff in England and the Chesapeake Colonies, 1607–1689.* Chapel Hill: University of North Carolina, Chapel Hill, 1930.

Kaufman County Historical Commission. *History of Kaufman County,* Vols. 1 and 2. Kaufman, Texas: National Share Graphics, 1957.

Keating, Bern. *An Illustrated History of the Texas Rangers.* Chicago: Rand McNally, 1975.

Kelcher, William A. *Violence in Lincoln County: 1869–1881.* Albuquerque: University of New Mexico Press, 1957.

Key, Della. *In the Cattle Country: History of Potter County, 1887–1966.* Wichita Falls: Nortex Offset Publications, 1972.

Kilgore, D. E. *A Ranger Legacy.* Austin: Madrona Press, 1973.

Kelling, George L., and Catherine M. Coles. *Fixing Broken Windows: Restoring Order and Reducing Crime in Our Communities.* New York: Simon & Schuster, 1996.

Laake, Doris G. *The History of Paige and Vicinity.* Austin: Eakin Publishers, 1983.

Lack, Paul D. *The Texas Revolutionary Experience: A Political and Social History 1835–1836.* College Station: Texas A & M Press, 1992.

Larson, Carole. *Forgotten Frontier, the Story of Southeastern New Mexico.* Albuquerque: University of New Mexico Press, 1993.

Livingston, William, editor. *Magna Carta.* Austin: LBJ Library, University of Texas, 1987.

McCarty, John. *Maverick Town: The Story of Old Tascosa*. Norman: University of Oklahoma Press, 1988.

McGrath, Roger D. *Gunfighters, Highwaymen, and Vigilantes: Violence on the Frontier*. Berkeley: University of California Press, 1984.

Martin, James. *Texas Divided: Loyalty and Dissent in the Lone Star State 1856–1874*. Lexington: University Press of Kentucky, 1990.

Metz, Leon C. *Dallas Stoudenmire, El Paso Marshal*. Norman: University of Oklahoma Press, 1979.

———. *John Selman, Gunfighter*. Norman: University of Oklahoma Press, 1980.

———. *John Wesley Hardin: Dark Angel of Texas*. El Paso: Mangan Books, 1996.

———. *Pat Garrett: The Story of a Western Lawman*. Norman: University of Oklahoma Press, 1973.

———. "Why Old John Selman Died." *Frontier Times* (November 1965):30–65.

Miller, Nyle H., and Joseph W. Snell. *Great Gunfighters of the Kansas Cowtowns 1867–1886*. Lincoln: University of Nebraska Press, 1967.

Miller, Rick. *Bounty Hunter*. College Station: Creative Publishing, 1988.

Morris, William Alfred. *The Medieval Sheriff to 1300*. Barnes and Noble, New York, 1968.

Morris, W. R. *The Legacy of Buford Pusser*. Paducah: Turner Publishing, 1994.

Newton, Lewis W. and Herbert P. Gambrell. *A Social & Political History of Texas*. Dallas: Turner, 1935.

Nueces County Historical Society. *The History of Nueces County*. Austin: Jenkins, 1972.

Nunn, W. C. *Texas Under the Carpetbaggers*. Austin: University of Texas Press, 1962.

O'Neal, Bill. *Encyclopedia of Western Gunfighters*. Norman: University of Oklahoma Press, 1979.

———. *Henry Brown, The Outlaw Marshal*. College Station: Creative Publishing, 1980.

Pingenot, Ben E. *Siringo*. College Station: Texas A & M Press, 1989.

Prassel, Frank Richard. *The Western Peace Officer: A Legacy of Law and Order*. Norman: University of Oklahoma Press, 1972.

Raine, William MacLeod. *Famous Sheriffs and Western Outlaws*. New York: Doubleday, Doran, 1929.

Ray, Worth S. *Austin Colony Pioneers*. Bastrop, Texas: Genealogical Publishing, 1995.

Raymond, Dora Nell. *Captain Lee Hall of Texas*. Norman: University of Oklahoma Press, 1940.

Richardson, Rupert, Adrian Anderson, and Ernest Wallace. *Texas, The Lone Star State*. New York: Prentice Hall, 1997.

Richter, William L. *The Army in Texas During Reconstruction, 1865–1870*. College Station: Texas A & M University Press, 1987.

Rigler, Lewis C., and Judith W. Rigler. *In the Line of Duty*. Denton: University of North Texas Press, 1995.

Rister, Carl Coke. *Fort Griffin on the Texas Frontier*. Norman: University of Oklahoma Press, 1956.

———. "The Rio Grande Colony" *Southwest Review* 25(July 1940).

Robertson, Pauline, and R. L. Robertson. *Panhandle Pilgrimage: Illustrated Tales Tracing History in the Texas Panhandle*. Amarillo: Paramount, 1976.

Roman, Mark. "The Cop Who Caught His Killers." *Reader's Digest* November 1993:67–72.

Rosa, Joseph G. *The Gunfighter: Man or Myth?* Norman: University of Oklahoma Press, 1969.

———. *They Called Him Wild Bill: The Life and Adventures of James Butler Hickok.* Norman: University of Oklahoma Press, 1964.

———. *The West of Wild Bill Hickok.* Norman: University of Oklahoma, 1982.

Rowe, E. "The Disturbances at Anahuac in 1832." *Texas State Historical Association Quarterly* 6(4)April 1903:265–99.

Selman, John, Jr. "John Selman," as told to F. Reynolds; *All Western Magazine* (October 1935):44–61.

Sitton, Thad. *Texas High Sheriffs.* Austin: Texas Monthly Press, 1988.

Smith, Dick. *Units of Local Government in Texas.* Austin: Bureau of Municipal Research, University of Texas, 1941.

Smithwick, Noah. *The Evolution of a State or Recollections of Old Texas Days.* Austin: University of Texas Press, 1983.

Sonnichsen, C. L. *Pass of the North: Four Centuries on the Rio Grande.* El Paso: Texas Western Press, 1968.

Sowell, A. J. *Rangers and Pioneers of Texas.* Austin: State House Press, 1991, originally published by author 1884.

Spikes, Nellie, and Temple Ann Ellis. *A History of Crosby County, Texas.* San Antonio: Naylor, 1952.

State Archives Division, "Compiled Index to Elected and Appointed Officials of the Republic of Texas: 1835-1846." Texas State Library, Austin, 1981.

Steen, Ralph W. *Twentieth Century Texas.* Austin: The Steck Company, 1942.

Sterling, William Warren. *Trails and Trials of a Texas Ranger.* Norman: University of Oklahoma Press, 1959.

Stiff, Edward, *The Texan Emigrant: A Narration of the Adventures of the Author in Texas, and a Description of the Soil, Climate, Productions, Minerals, Towns, Bays, Harbors, Rivers, Institutions, and Manners and Customs of the Inhabitants of that Country in 1840.* Austin: Texian Press, 1968.

Stovall, Allan V. *Breaks of the Balcones, A Regional History.* Barksdale: privately published by Allan Stovall, 1967.

Taylor, William C. *A History of Clay County.* Austin: Jenkins Publishing Co., 1972.

Tefertiller, Casey. *Wyatt Earp: The Life Behind the Legend.* New York: John Wiley & Son, 1997.

Tyler, George W. *The History of Bell County.* San Antonio: Naylor Co., 1936.

Wallace, Ernest, David M. Vigness, and George B. Ward, Editors. *Documents of Texas History.* Austin: State House Press, 1994.

Webb, Walter Prescott. *The Story of the Texas Rangers.* Austin: Encino Press, 1957.

———. *The Texas Rangers: A Century of Frontier Defense.* New York: Houghton Mifflin Company, 1935.

Weems, John Edward, and Jane Weems. *Dreams of Empire, A Human History of the Republic of Texas.* New York: Simon & Schuster, 1971.

Wellman, Paul I. *A Dynasty of Western Outlaws.* New York: Bonanza Books, 1961.

Wilbanks, William. *Forgotten Heroes: Police Officers Killed in Bell County, 1850–1994.* Belton: Bell County Museum, 1995.

———. *Forgotten Heroes: Police Officers Killed in Dade County.* Paducah: Turner Publishing, 1996.

———. *Forgotten Heroes: Police Officers Killed in Greenville County.* Paducah: Turner Publishing, 1997.

Williams, Clayton W., *Texas' Last Frontier: Fort Stockton and the Trans-Pecos, 1861-1898.* College Station: Texas A & M University Press, 1982.

Williams, John Hoyt. *Sam Houston: The Life & Times of the Liberator of Texas, an Authentic American Hero.* New York: Simon & Schuster, 1993.

Williams, Marjorie L., editor. *Fayette County: Past and Present.* La Grange: Marjorie Williams, 1976.

Wilkins, Fredrick. *The Legend Begins: The Texas Rangers 1823–1845.* Austin: State House Press, 1996.

NEWSPAPERS

Alice Daily Echo
Corpus Christi Caller & Daily Herald
Corpus Christi Times
Fort Worth Star-Telegram
Jasper Newsboy
The Monitor, McAllen, Texas
Pittsburg Gazette
Pleasanton Express
San Antonio Express-News
Temple Daily Telegram
Williamson County Sun

AUDIO-VIDEO

Videotape made on 1-23-91, in patrol car of Constable Darrell Lunsford.

INTERVIEWS

There were numerous individuals and organizations interviewed during the research and writing of this book. Some of those interviewed did not provide information applicable to the stories contained in the book, but many did. Identification of those persons whose interviews were used are contained in the notes or are identified in the acknowledgments.

ARCHIVAL MATERIAL

The Austin Papers, Center for American History University of Texas, Austin.
Bexar Archives, Center for American History, University of Texas, Austin.
Court Records, County Clerk's offices in Bexar, Colorado, Fort Bend, Fayette, Nacogdoches, Nueces, Potter, Washington, and Williamson counties.
Election Records, Texas State Archives and Library, Austin.
Texas Ranger archives, Texas State Archives and Library, Austin.
Archival material at Texas Ranger Hall of Fame Museum, Waco.
Texas State Police archives, Texas State Archives and Library, Austin.

Index

All towns and counties named in the index are in Texas unless otherwise indicated.